TOAST

A TOAST to the HOME COOK

MIKE GARCIA
AND SHAHRAM BIJAN

with LESLIE HARLIB

Shahram Bijan
Toast Novato
5800 Nave Drive, Unit G
Novato, CA 94949
(415) 382-1144

Photographs by Leo Gong and Rien van Rijthoven
Design by Preston Thomas
Proofread by Laura Iwasaki

ISBN 978-0-615-40355-7

Printed in the United States of America

First edition, October 2010

BRIEF CONTENTS

CONTENTS

BIOS

The Owner

Shahram Bijan took an unusual route to becoming a restaurateur, one that involved a family passion, an international move, the high-tech industry, and a heartfelt dream.

He grew up in Iran and moved to the United States with his parents in the 1980s. When he was eighteen, he and three partners founded an Internet start-up company, which was later bought out by a larger company. By the time he was nineteen, he had enough resources to follow his bliss.

A core value in Shahram's family was spending quality time together over good food. That value became the essence of what his future would hold. He welded his innate sense of hospitality to his fascination with cuisine and plunged into the restaurant business.

Shahram bought First Crush, a San Francisco wine bar and restaurant, in 2001. Within six months, he'd revamped everything, and the restaurant took off. First Crush has since won many Wine Spectator and Wine Enthusiast awards and has been recognized by OpenTable and CitySearch. It is highly rated by Zagat and has been featured on Rachael Ray's television show. After building it into one of the Union Square area's most successful dining destinations, Shahram started looking to develop other restaurants.

Toast, a small and vibrant restaurant on Sunnyside Avenue in Mill Valley, caught his attention. With Chef Mike Garcia heading the kitchen, Toast made a success of serving American and globally inspired comfort food. This restaurant did so well that Shahram was inspired to offer the concept to a larger audience. So he opened Toast Novato in the new Hamilton Marketplace in 2009. This Toast is more than twice the size of his Mill Valley restaurant and was created from the ground up to his specifications. The people of Novato welcomed Toast warmly. Both restaurants built a loyal following from around the Bay Area as well as in their own neighborhoods.

With so much positive response, Shahram decided it was his turn to give back. Here are more than 125 cherished recipes from Toast that you can now make in the comfort of your own home.

The Chef

I come from a family whose love of food inspired my grandmother to open two restaurants in the mid-1940s. My grandfather was a pantry chef on the Presidential Cruise Line before World War II, and my mother developed beautiful skills as a cook that always warmed the heart of our family when I was growing up.

So with all that good food around me, I guess it was natural that I loved to cook, even as a child. I'd often prepare meals for my parents, and they daringly tried whatever I created. I remember once trying to make a pizza with flour, water, and salt. It came out pretty much like crunchy Play-Doh, but my father sat down and ate it for lunch! I've always appreciated that support.

Drawing and painting were passions of mine as well, and later, sculpture — mainly ice sculpture — became a big part of my life. This is probably why I fell so much in love with cooking, which is a multidimensional form of art. Smell, feel, taste, and presentation are my materials, whether I'm cooking for my family or catering for 850 people. It's always rewarding, and I love what I do.

The past twenty-five years of working in kitchens, starting as a dishwasher for a local caterer, have given me time to continually hone my skills, often through a lot of trial and error. So don't be afraid to try new things. If a dish doesn't work the first time, it will turn out right on the second or even the third try. Cooking is about feeling. It's about not only what you are cooking but how you are cooking it, who you are cooking for, and where you are cooking. All of these elements impart flavor to your food as well as bring family and friends together to celebrate life around it.

I would like to dedicate this book to my family — my children, Julia, Callie, Matteo, and Leia, and my beautiful wife, Nicole.

CHEF MICHAEL GARCIA

The Food Writer

Leslie Harlib has been a food journalist and restaurant columnist for more than twenty-five years, with columns in the *Village Voice, San Francisco Bay Guardian, San Francisco Weekly,* and *San Francisco Downtown.* For ten years, she was the staff food writer and restaurant critic for the *Marin Independent Journal,* the daily newspaper serving Marin County, California. She is currently the dining columnist for the Marinscope chain of newspapers and does public relations and marketing work for a variety of clients, from restaurants to independent businesses. Leslie is also an accomplished saloon pianist and singer who has performed her way around the world on cruise ships and in various international cities. She lives in San Rafael, California, with three cats, two dogs, a bird, and several hundred cookbooks. Contact her at lharlib@gmail.com and www.leslieharlib.com.

THANKS

SHAHRAM WOULD LIKE TO THANK THE FOLLOWING PEOPLE:

This book would not have been possible without the dedication and commitment of the many people who have made Toast so successful.

First, I would like to thank my family for their unwavering support and belief in me. To my mom, who has always been my rock and my biggest cheerleader, thank you for helping me in all the ways that you do and encouraging me to express myself. To my dad, whose knowledge and amazing cooking skills gave me the inspiration to get into the restaurant industry, I thank you for all of your support and wisdom. To the rest of my family, thank you for honoring my process and always believing in me.

To my beautiful wife, Brittany, who endured long hours, even days, without seeing me and who dealt with the stress and craziness of the business, thank you for standing by my side and keeping me grounded when I needed you most. I love you. To my two children, Shaia and Gianna, when I see your beautiful faces at the end of the day, you energize me to get up and do it again tomorrow.

To all my restaurant staff, without you, none of this would be possible. Your passion and dedication are what make the restaurants so successful. Without your commitment, it would be impossible to achieve what we have achieved.

To Leslie, Preston, and Laura, without your experience and guidance, this book would be just a bunch of words on paper.

To Stanley and Alan, thank you for your incredible vision and brilliant design, which brought Toast to life.

A special thanks to Mike, who has been not only an unbelievable chef but a dedicated friend who really believed in Toast and helped make it what it is today. I hope we continue to work together for many more years and take Toast to new heights.

And most important, to all of the patrons who have allowed us to live out our dream, I can't thank you enough for your continued support and loyalty. You've become a second family to many of us, and we are so grateful.

SHAHRAM BIJAN

MIKE WOULD LIKE TO THANK THE FOLLOWING PEOPLE:

What a long strange trip it's been from our beginning in 2003, when we opened the café-style Mill Valley restaurant. This restaurant concept was new to me. All the restaurants I'd worked in before had been white-tablecloth style or in luxury hotels. At Toast, I discovered that I really liked the more casual, down-to-earth setting. I was able to throw in creative twists and upscale cooking techniques and come up with dishes that people really appreciated.

At Toast, I also had the chance to meet and talk to a lot of our neighborhood customers, getting to know them and their families as they got to know mine.

Toast developed into a neighborhood and family-oriented place that serves wholesome and comforting food. We built a loyal following and looked for another small place where we could expand our audience. But we got lucky and found a huge space, with 200-plus seats, in Novato. And we were lucky with timing, too, because the trend of good-quality comfort food was taking off in America.

Then came the writing, development, and completion of this book, *A Toast to the Home Cook.*

It's amazing what you can do when you believe in something. None of this would have been accomplished without the dedication and hard work of my staff, especially the ones who have been with me from the beginning. They are the people who turn our vision of our restaurants into reality, day after day.

I would like to thank the Toast managers for fully supporting me, both in the restaurants and in creating this book.

I'd like to thank Leslie and Laura for taking my roughly written cookbook and turning it into something everyone can understand.

A special thanks to my family for understanding what it means to be a chef/restaurateur and supporting me by giving me the time and dedication I need to be good at what I do.

I would also like to thank my friend and partner, Shahram Bijan, without whom none of this would have been possible.

MICHAEL GARCIA

INTRO

Do you remember your favorite childhood food?

I was raised in a Persian household with exotic delights culled from my dad's family heritage and his trips around the world. His creations were similar to what you'd find in a fine-dining restaurant. So at a very young age, I was exposed to a level of cuisine that many do not experience until adulthood.

My father's passion for food was a siren's song that drew many people to congregate at our house, where gatherings of more than a hundred were a monthly occurrence. He took great pride in planning the menu and shopping for unique ingredients. Pomegranates, curries, special fish, lamb, and loads of fresh herbs were natural to me. Yet for every person who came to dinner, there were kids I knew who had never heard of such foods and were hesitant to try anything as odd-sounding as a pomegranate.

After exploring different fields in which to make my mark, I found I always returned to food. My father's passion became my passion, and I embarked on owning my own restaurant, now several of them. I wanted my restaurants to combine the casual feel of my parents' parties with culinary excellence. I visited competing restaurants often and always found a table when a new restaurant blipped onto the radar. I wanted to stay on top of the newest trends and take in as much knowledge about fine-dining food as possible. So I traveled, and I ate, always going for the dish I hadn't heard of or the menu item that seemed the most adventurous.

Yet, for me, the meaning of a really good meal always came back to my childhood favorite — lamb stew, which was much more rewarding, more comforting than any of the fancier dishes I tried. Food done simply and well can be more satisfying than dishes made up of so many ingredients that you forget what their essence is all about. There is an inherent intimidation factor in fine dining. The decor, the wait staff, and the menu all influence the need to feel comfort, the need to feel that you belong.

But put a steaming, golden-crusted chicken pot pie in front of someone, and you can almost see the body relax. Break open the crust and find big chunks of chicken breast, carrots, and herbs cloaked in a rich creamy sauce, and it's almost impossible to wait for it to cool before you take that first bite. I wanted people to have that experience when they visit my restaurants. I wanted them to feel like they were home, that they were being cared for and comforted.

Toast is straightforward, yet it is an integral part of many people's every-day experience. There is no better feeling than to overhear someone rave about an amazing meal and then mention your restaurant. Like music or your favorite scent, simple rustic dishes tend to evoke strong emotions. They take you back to memories of your mom warming you up with a hearty meal after you were out all day playing in the fog, the buttery goodness of the grilled cheese sandwich and the salty richness of the tomato soup making the sting of the cold disappear. Remember the cool trickle of watermelon juice down your parched throat after a hot day at the park? When you bite into a chunk of watermelon in a salad, its juicy sweetness can take you right back to that moment.

Mike Garcia, like me, lives for those moments. It was a natural progression for him to head the kitchen at Toast. He is a family man and, like my father, has a passion for food. He wanted to keep Toast's fare simple while using high-quality ingredients and as many organic, locally grown items as possible. Mike created a menu that appeals to a variety of palates but has a universal theme — comfort. He wanted people to walk into his dining room and smell Mom's pot roast, Auntie's fried chicken, Dad's barbecue.

Through our experiences at Toast, we have found pleasure and happiness in our lives, and we want to share those feelings with you. In this book, in his own words, Mike shares his recipes for dishes that have brought us warmth and joy. We hope you will find the same when you cook them. Perhaps one of these dishes will even become a family favorite.

PANCAKES, WAFFLES, FRENCH TOAST

PANCAKES, WAFFLES, FRENCH TOAST

To me, a steaming hot stack of pancakes dripping with melted butter and real maple syrup defines comfort food. Pancakes were always my favorite when I was growing up. They'd be served on Sundays or on special mornings. I remember how happy I felt as a kid, waking up and seeing a platter of hot pancakes on the table with a pile of crisp bacon next to them. The kitchen would smell heavenly with the warm scents of syrup and frying pork. It's fun to try different flavors with your pancakes and waffles, such as assorted fruits or types of syrup other than maple. I've given you some basic ideas so you can really start to have fun with fillings and toppings.

BASIC PANCAKES

Makes 4 8-inch pancakes

I'd like to show you how to prepare a basic pancake batter and how to cook pancakes for the best results.

Learning to prepare a basic recipe opens the door to a whole world of creative ideas for amazing pancakes — think of hotcakes enhanced with fresh fruit or chocolate chips, savory pancakes, and pancakes enriched with healthful fiber.

If you don't have time to make a batter from scratch (many of us are strapped for time), use one of your favorite mixes and adjust the ingredients a little. Most store-bought brands yield a batter that I find a bit dense, so I would add a little more baking powder and a little sugar to try and achieve a light, fluffy pancake.

Cast iron griddles seem to work the best for browning the cakes, giving them a slightly crisp texture on the outside while keeping them fluffy in the middle. Any other griddle should work fine, though. If you don't have a griddle, use a 12-inch nonstick pan. The trick is to have enough room to flip each pancake. By the way, the following recipe will also make great buttermilk pancakes; just subsitute 1/2 cup buttermilk for 1/2 cup milk.

What You Need

Cast iron griddle or 12-inch or larger nonstick pan   Spatula   Mixing bowl
Whisk   4-ounce ladle

How to Make

1. Mix the dry ingredients in a large bowl.
2. Add milk, eggs, vanilla, and oil and mix well. Let batter sit for a few minutes.
3. Meanwhile, heat griddle over medium-high heat and rub generously with canola oil. Sprinkle some water droplets on the griddle; if you get a good sizzle, it's ready to go.
4. With the ladle, pour circles of batter onto the griddle.
5. Cook until the edges are browning and large bubbles form in the center of the cakes.
6. With a sturdy spatula, flip each pancake and cook on the other side for about a minute.
7. If cakes are too light, increase the heat slightly; if they're too dark, lower the heat until you get the desired browning.
8. Top with butter, powdered sugar, and a little maple syrup.

Ingredients

1-1/2 cups all-purpose flour
2 tablespoons granulated sugar
1-1/2 tablespoons baking powder
1/2 teaspoon baking soda
Pinch salt
1-1/4 cups milk (for buttermilk pancakes, subsitute 1/2 cup buttermilk for 1/2 cup milk)
2 eggs
1 teaspoon pure vanilla extract
2 teaspoons canola oil plus more for cooking

CREATIVE PANCAKES

Makes 4 8-inch pancakes

Now that you understand basic pancakes, here are some more ideas for easy creative pancakes that showcase fresh fruits of the season, nuts, candies, cereals, and dried fruits. You can also be creative with toppings: Consider fruit compotes, fruit purées, Nutella, honey, whipped cream, ricotta, etc.

GREAT ADDITIONS:

Fresh fruit: Blueberries, bananas, strawberries, sliced mangos, apples, pineapple

Nuts: Walnuts, pecans, macadamia nuts

Dried fruit: Raisins, cranberries, dates, apricots — any type of dried fruit

Spices and crunchies: Cinnamon, granola, Rice Krispies, shredded coconut

Candies: Chocolate chips, crushed Heath Bar, chopped Snickers, chopped peanut brittle, M&Ms

What You Need

Cast iron griddle or 12-inch or larger nonstick pan   Spatula   Mixing bowl
Whisk   4-ounce ladle

How to Make

As you are making the Basic Pancakes (either regular or buttermilk), sprinkle the flavoring of your choice on top of each pancake right after you ladle it onto the griddle. Keep in mind that these are still pancakes. Don't overload them with ingredients.

FLANNEL PANCAKE

This is one very popular pancake at our restaurants. It contains granola and wheat germ, which give each cake a little crunchy texture. And it's a good way to add extra fiber to your diet. Top this version with fresh fruit and a drizzle of honey.

PUMPKIN-PECAN PANCAKES

Serves 4 to 8

Autumn is one of the best times of the year to make pancakes, because with that chill in the air, the cakes freshly steaming from the griddle seem to warm you from the inside out. This particular recipe enhances the feel of the season with a taste that evokes pumpkin pie. At the restaurants, we usually serve them in October and November, athough they're so popular that people request them year-round.

In this recipe, I use a little more baking powder to counterbalance the density of the pumpkin purée. (You still want your pancakes light and fluffy.) To simplify this recipe, substitute your favorite instant pancake batter and use spiced pumpkin purée. When it comes to the nuts, candied pecans taste the best here, but you can substitute plain roasted pecans as well. Serve these bronze, fragrant cakes with pecan butter and pure maple syrup.

What You Need

Food processor   Griddle   Mixing bowl   4-ounce ladle

How to Make

FOR THE PECAN BUTTER:

Place all ingredients in the food processor and pulse till well mixed. Remove to a small bowl or container, cover, and refrigerate. Keeps in the refrigerator for up to 3 weeks.

FOR THE PANCAKES:

1. Prepare the buttermilk version of the Basic Pancakes batter.
2. Add pumpkin purée, spice mix, and baking powder.
3. Heat the griddle over medium heat and rub with canola oil. When griddle is hot, sprinkle with a few drops of water — if they bead and sizzle, you're ready to go.
4. Ladle out pancakes and top with pecans.
5. Flip when brown, about 4 minutes, and cook until they look fluffy, another 3 to 4 minutes.
6. Rub more oil onto the griddle before ladling out each new batch of pancakes.
7. When cakes are done, top with pecan butter and serve immediately.

Ingredients

For the pecan butter (makes about 3/4 cup):

1/2 cup (1 stick) unsalted butter, softened

1/2 cup pecans

2 tablespoons honey

Pinch salt

For the pancakes:

2 batches Basic Pancakes batter, buttermilk version (recipe, p. 6)

1/2 cup canned pumpkin purée

1 tablespoon pumpkin pie spice mix

1 teaspoon baking powder

1/4 cup canola oil

1 cup chopped, candied pecans (see Candied Walnuts, p. 222)

1/4 cup pecan butter

COCONUT MACADAMIA PANCAKES WITH PINEAPPLE-MANGO COMPOTE

Makes 4 8-inch pancakes

This tropical pancake is a favorite at our restaurants during summer months. Served with a fruit compote instead of syrup, it makes for a beautiful presentation and sparkles with exotic flavors.

Make sure the fruit is ripe before making the compote. Smelling the fruit is the best way to judge ripeness. If you are able to smell the natural sweetness and almost taste the fruit through its aroma, it's ready to use. The compote can be prepared a day ahead so the actual preparation of the pancakes is fast and easy.

What You Need

2-quart saucepan   Mixing bowl   Pancake griddle   4-ounce ladle

How to Make

FOR THE COMPOTE

1. In the saucepan, combine Coco Lopez, granulated sugar, and fruit juice and reduce* over medium heat until the sauce is thick and syrupy, about 4 to 5 minutes. It needs to be good and thick before you add the fruit, or it will become watery.
2. Once the right consistency is reached, add the mango and pineapple and cook until the fruit releases its juices, about 4 minutes.
3. Mix cornstarch with cold water. Stir into the compote and cook about 2 more minutes. If the syrup looks too thick, add a little water. Let cool; then refrigerate.

FOR THE PANCAKES

1. Heat the griddle over medium heat.
2. When griddle is hot enough (a drop of water will sizzle on it), grease it with butter, ladle on the Basic Pancakes batter, and top each cake with macadamia nuts and coconut.
3. When pancakes are brown on one side, flip them over and quickly sear the other side. Be sure not to burn the coconut.
4. When pancakes are done, top them with the compote, coconut, more macadamia nuts, and powdered sugar.

*See "chop," "dice," and "reduce" in the Glossary; for toasting, see Tips and Techniques.

Ingredients

1/4 cup Coco Lopez (sweet coconut syrup), stirred well
4 tablespoons granulated sugar
1 cup mango or pineapple juice
3 cups diced* fresh mango
2 cups diced fresh pineapple
1 teaspoon cornstarch
1 teaspoon cold water
Basic Pancakes batter (recipe, p. 6), substituting coconut milk for regular milk
Butter
1 cup toasted,* chopped* macadamia nuts
2 cups toasted, sweetened shredded coconut
1/4 cup powdered sugar

LEMON-RICOTTA PANCAKES

Serves 4

How about pancakes that are light and fluffy and feature a lemony tang? They're so flavorful, they don't even need syrup. I usually use fresh fruit purée (such as raspberry) as a garnish, along with a spoonful of ricotta cheese and a few fresh berries.

When folding the egg whites into the batter, it's important to gently fold, not stir. This style of pancake batter can be used in a lot of different ways, with many flavorings and garnishes: it's entirely up to you. If you can find Meyer lemons, use them for an even more complex flavor.

What You Need

3 mixing bowls   Griddle   Whisk   Hand-held electric beater

How to Make

1. In a large bowl, mix together flour, sugar, baking powder, salt, and nutmeg.
2. In another bowl, mix 3 egg yolks with lemon zest, lemon juice, buttermilk, milk, water, lemon extract, and vanilla extract.
3. Combine the wet and dry ingredients in the larger bowl.
4. Gently add ricotta.
5. In a separate, clean bowl, beat 3 egg whites until they form soft peaks. (A copper bowl is the best one to use because it gives the egg whites more fluff.)
6. Carefully fold egg whites into the batter.
7. Heat the griddle, rub with canola oil, ladle on batter, and cook pancakes until they are golden brown on both sides.
8. Keep the pancakes in a warm oven (around 200F) until ready to serve.

Ingredients

2-1/4 cups all-purpose flour
1/4 cup granulated sugar
2-1/2 tablespoons baking powder
1 teaspoon salt
1/2 teaspoon nutmeg
3 large eggs, separated
    (make sure eggs are at
    room temperature)
1/4 cup lemon zest
3 tablespoons lemon juice
1 cup buttermilk
1-1/4 cups milk
1/4 cup water
2 tablespoons lemon extract
2 teaspoons pure vanilla extract
2 tablespoons ricotta
1/4 cup canola oil

WAFFLES

Serves 4

Waffles are always a treat, thick and crisp, with pockets on their surface to catch all that luscious butter and syrup.

The basic batter is simple to make. For fun variations, add different flavors to the waffles, such as chopped cooked bacon, chocolate chips, assorted nuts, ground cinnamon, finely diced apple, or a little malt. You can even add 3 tablespoons of cocoa powder to make chocolate waffles. The list of different toppings and fillings can go on and on. I usually top these waffles with butter, fresh berries, and whipped cream and serve with a side of pure maple syrup.

The waffle iron itself is a key component. There are some pretty good, reasonably priced waffle irons out there. Try to find a nonstick version with thick, heavy waffle areas, ideally one that rotates so that both sides of the waffle cook evenly.

What You Need

Waffle iron   Mixing bowl   Whisk   Ladle

How to Make

1. Heat the waffle iron according to the instructions. Each iron works differently, but essentially, if you want crisper waffles, turn the heat up higher. Conversely, if you like your waffle less crunchy, lower the heat.
2. In the bowl, mix together all the dry ingredients.
3. Add buttermilk, eggs, milk, melted butter, and vanilla extract and whisk very well until there are no lumps.
4. Let batter sit for 30 minutes.
5. Open the hot waffle iron and coat well with PAM cooking spray or brush with melted butter. Ladle in the batter — usually 4 ounces is enough (if there's too much batter, it will overflow and make a big mess).
6. Cook until the waffle is golden brown and crisp.
7. Remove carefully and serve immediately.

*See "PAM cooking spray" in the Glossary.

Ingredients

2 cups flour
3 teaspoons baking powder
1/2 teaspoon salt
1 teaspoon baking soda
2 teaspoons granulated sugar
2 cups buttermilk
2 extra-large eggs
1-1/2 cups milk
6 tablespoons melted unsalted butter
1 tablespoon pure vanilla extract
PAM cooking spray* or melted butter

CRISPY FRIED FRENCH TOAST

Makes 10 pieces

This is the crispiest French toast you will ever eat. Because it's so rich, serve small portions. It also works well as a dessert topped with raisin rum ice cream or bananas Foster and vanilla ice cream. For breakfast, top the toast with sliced bananas, strawberries, blueberries, butter, and powdered sugar and/or maple syrup. Serve with a side of chicken apple sausage.

What You Need

Griddle or 12-inch nonstick pan   Sheet pan   Deep-sided skillet or deep-fryer
Ovenproof platter

Ingredients

Basic Pancakes batter
    (recipe, p. 6)
1/2 cup water
1 teaspoon cinnamon
1/2 teaspoon ground nutmeg
1/2 cup canola oil
5 pieces Texas toast cut in half
    or thick-cut sourdough bread

How to Make

1. Add water, cinnamon, and nutmeg to Basic Pancakes batter.
2. Heat griddle over medium-high heat until it smokes lightly. Add 2 to 3 tablespoons of oil to the pan.
3. Dip bread in pancake batter to coat. Place in pan and cook for only a few seconds on each side, just to seal the batter on the bread.
4. Set bread pieces aside on sheet pan.
5. Heat the skillet over medium-high heat. Add oil to a depth of at least 1/4 inch, enough to fry in.
6. When oil is hot (it should start to smoke), put in a couple of slices of batter-coated bread and fry* until they are crisp and golden brown on both sides, about 2 minutes per side.
7. Pat dry on paper towels and keep warm on a platter in a low oven (around 200F) until ready to serve.

*For frying, see Tips and Techniques.

CINNAMON FRENCH TOAST

Serves 4

To me, the aromas of cinnamon French toast and bacon cooking in the morning help create a feeling of warmth and family. It's a cozy, filling way to start the day, and it is so easy to do.

This is our version of a classic American staple. We use brioche for this recipe because it has so much deep, eggy flavor. But if you can't find brioche loaf, thick slices of Texas toast will work well. Top with pecan butter (see Pumpkin-Pecan Pancakes, p. 9), fresh berries, a side of whipped cream, and your favorite maple syrup and, of course, serve with a side of bacon.

What You Need

Mixing bowl   Deep-sided 12-inch skillet   Whisk   Ovenproof platter

How to Make

1. In the mixing bowl, whisk eggs; then add cream, orange juice, vanilla, sugar, zest, salt, and spices. Let the batter sit for a few minutes.
2. In the skillet, add oil to a depth of 1/4 inch; turn heat to medium high.
3. When oil begins to smoke lightly, dip the bread in the batter. Make sure it soaks, fully covered, for 3 or 4 seconds on each side. Don't let it sit too long or it will turn to mush.
4. Lay the bread in the pan. You should hear a sizzle when you put the slices in. Do not crowd them; give yourself room to work.
5. Cook toasts until brown and crispy, about 3 minutes per side. If they are getting too dark, turn down the heat a little. If they seem too oily, turn up the heat a little. Each slice should take around 6 minutes to cook.
6. Once both sides are browned, remove from the skillet and pat dry on paper towels.
7. Keep slices warm on a platter in the oven at low heat (200F).
8. Repeat with remaining bread, adding a little more oil with each batch if needed and removing leftover bits and pieces as you go.
9. When all slices are done, serve immediately.

Ingredients

6 eggs
1 egg yolk
1 cup heavy cream
1/2 cup orange juice
2 tablespoons pure vanilla extract
1/4 cup granulated sugar
1 tablespoon orange zest
Pinch salt
1 tablespoon ground cinnamon
1/2 teaspoon ground nutmeg
3/4 cup canola oil
8 slices bread about 1-inch thick, cut in half diagonally

EGGS, OMELETS, SCRAMBLES

EGGS, OMELETS, SCRAMBLES

Eggs are a staple on American breakfast tables. Nothing says "Good morning" better than a skillet of hot scrambled eggs with cheese or a fluffy omelet brimming with luscious ingredients. Many people think eggs are a snap to make, but they're surprisingly easy to mess up, so the trick is to pay close attention to the timing. Using organic eggs makes a huge difference to the overall pleasure of eating eggs because their flavor is richer. When making omelets, strive for light and fluffy textures. Having all your ingredients ready before you start cooking is essential. Eggs cook so quickly that you need to be prepared. Once you have mastered some of these recipes, get creative and dream up some of your own.

HUEVOS RANCHEROS

Serves 4

This is a classic dish. Every chef and home cook has his or her own way of doing it. It's a snap to assemble, but it does take time to prepare the components: the Ranchero Sauce, Salsa Fresca, and Black Beans. Mind you, all these elements can be prepared beforehand. You can even make the sauce and beans a couple of weeks ahead and freeze in small batches.

The type of tortilla you use makes a big difference here as well. I think soft corn tortillas work best. They're available at local Mexican groceries.

Adding grilled steak, chicken, or chorizo turns this dish into a hearty breakfast.

What You Need

8-inch nonstick frying pan   2 2-quart saucepans

How to Make

Preheat oven to 375F.

1. Heat the Black Beans and the Ranchero Sauce in separate saucepans.
2. Warm tortillas in the oven.
3. Put 3 tortillas on each plate, overlapping each other. Cover tortillas with beans and the cheddar and jack cheeses and put the plates back in the oven for a few minutes to melt the cheeses a little.
4. In the pan, cook the eggs. Over easy works best with this dish because the runny yolks add other dimensions of flavor and texture. Use 2 eggs for each plate.
5. Top each pair of eggs with Ranchero Sauce, one-fourth of the sliced avocado, Salsa Fresca, 1 tablespoon of sour cream, crumbled Cotija cheese, cilantro sprigs, and a Roasted Jalapeño half.

Ingredients

2 cups Ranchero Sauce (recipe, p. 236)
3 cups Black Beans (recipe, p. 188)
12 soft corn tortillas
2 cups shredded mixed cheddar and jack cheeses
8 extra-large eggs
1 avocado
1/2 cup Salsa Fresca (recipe, p. 239)
4 tablespoons sour cream
1/4 cup Cotija cheese (found in Mexican markets)
Cilantro sprigs
4 halves Roasted Jalapeños (recipe, p. 203)

PESTO CHICKEN SCRAMBLE

Serves 1 to 2

It's amazing how well pesto and eggs go together; this recipe celebrates that marriage. The combination of shredded chicken, artichoke, asparagus, Roasted Tomato, and Parmesan and fontina cheeses is a hit as well. Cooking it with eggs in this elaborate scramble really brings the flavors together.

Fresh artichoke hearts are the way to go if you're willing to take the time. Just boil the artichokes whole, pull off the leaves (cutting off the tender part of the center leaves), and then clean and slice the heart and stem. Otherwise, canned artichoke hearts in brine, not oil, or frozen ones would work, too. Fresh hot sourdough, Prosecco or other sparkling wine, baby greens with vinaigrette, and some crisp red grapes would round out this luscious meal.

What You Need

10-inch nonstick frying pan   Whisk   Rubber spatula or wooden spoon
Mixing bowl

How to Make

1. Heat the frying pan to medium high; add oil.
2. When oil begins to smoke, add the onion. Cook for about 2 minutes until onion begins to sweat* and soften; then add asparagus and artichoke and continue to cook for another minute.
3. Add Roasted Tomato, chicken, and pine nuts.
4. Whisk eggs together with Pesto and add to pan. Stir mixture constantly with the rubber spatula for about 4 minutes.
5. When eggs start to thicken, add cheeses, salt, and pepper. Serve immediately.

*See "chop," "Parmesan," and "sweat" in the Glossary; for cutting on the bias and toasting, see Tips and Techniques.

Ingredients

2 tablespoons olive oil
2 tablespoons chopped* yellow onion
2 asparagus, cut into 2-inch pieces on the bias*
1/4 cup thinly sliced artichoke hearts
1 Roasted Tomato (recipe, p. 204), coarsely chopped
1/3 cup cooked, shredded chicken, both white and dark meat
1 tablespoon toasted* pine nuts
3 extra-large eggs
1 tablespoon Pesto (recipe, p. 235)
2 tablespoons grated Parmesan*
3 tablespoons shredded fontina cheese
Salt and pepper to taste

BASIC CHEESE OMELET

Makes 1 omelet

Making a really good omelet takes some practice, so I always suggest starting with a simple recipe like this one. It's not overloaded with ingredients, which makes it a snap to prepare.

There are many ways to make omelets. You can roll them up with everything in the middle, in the French style, or you can fold them over the filling like an American omelet. I usually put a couple of ingredients in the eggs to give the omelet some flavor and then wrap up the rest in the middle.

Before you start, here are a few pieces of advice. Whipping the eggs is very important; this lets in air and makes the eggs fluffier. It's also important to fluff the omelet while it's cooking. The type of pan is important, too. A 10-inch nonstick pan with a little weight to it works best for me. And finally, keep the heat down: eggs burn easily.

What You Need

10-inch nonstick frying pan   Mixing bowl   Whisk   Small rubber spatula
Large spatula

Ingredients

3 large eggs
2 tablespoons clarified butter*
   or light olive oil
1/4 cup shredded Gruyère,
   cheddar, or jack cheese
Salt and pepper

How to Make

1. Heat the frying pan over medium heat for about 1 minute.
2. Crack the eggs into the bowl.
3. Add clarified butter to the pan and heat until it just begins to bubble.
4. Whip eggs vigorously with the whisk and immediately pour into the pan.
5. Cook the eggs until edges start to form, about 1 minute. Then, with a small rubber spatula, begin fluffing the omelet.* Continue doing this until there is no more runny egg.
6. Cook for 2 more seconds and then shake the pan to make sure the omelet is not sticking. If it is sticking, add a little more butter at the edge of the pan and slide the rubber spatula underneath to loosen the eggs.
7. Tilt the omelet away from you toward the edge of the pan and flip with the large spatula.
8. Sprinkle the cheese evenly over the omelet and follow with salt and pepper to taste. Cook for about 2 more seconds.
9. To plate, fold one-third of the omelet over with the rubber spatula and slide the omelet toward the plate. Roll it into another third and then slide onto the plate. This might take a little practice. Serve immediately.

*For clarified butter and fluffing an omelet, see Tips and Techniques.

CAJUN OMELET

Serves 1

Filled with spice and the flavor of Louisiana, this hearty omelet will take your taste buds straight to Bourbon Street. Obviously, Cajun spices are integral to this dish. You can either buy some or make a batch of your own and keep it on the spice rack. The main thing is to create that nice balance of heat and flavor. Crawfish meat, which I recommend for this recipe, is sometimes hard to come by, so substitute chopped prawns if you can't get crawfish.

    If you're making more than one omelet, simply increase the amount of filling accordingly and assemble the omelets one at a time. They go beautifully with warm Cornbread with Jalapeño and Cheddar (recipe, p. 183), sweet cream butter, and Crispy Potato Hash (recipe, p. 197)

What You Need

2 10-inch frying pans   Mixing bowl   Whisk   Rubber spatula

How to Make

1. Heat the frying pan over medium-high heat.
2. Add butter and andouille sausage. Cook for 2 to 3 minutes.
3. Add 2 tablespoons of onion, bell pepper, garlic, clam juice, tomato, 1/2 tablespoon of Cajun spices, and filé powder. Cook until the mixture starts to bind and thicken slightly.
4. Add crawfish, parsley, dash of Tabasco sauce, salt, and pepper. Stir for a couple of seconds just to warm. (Crawfish meat is already cooked when you buy it, so you don't want to overcook it. The same goes for the shrimp.)
5. Heat the pan. Add clarified butter, 1 tablespoon onion, and 1/2 tablespoon Cajun spices. Whisk eggs in the bowl and pour into the pan.
6. Fluff omelet;* then flip, sprinkle on the cheese, spoon sauce down the middle, and fold the omelet onto a plate.

*See "chop" and "dice" in the Glossary; for clarified butter and fluffing an omelet, see Tips and Techniques.

Ingredients

1 tablespoon unsalted butter
1/4 cup andouille sausage, diced* small
3 tablespoons finely chopped* yellow onion
2 tablespoons finely chopped green bell pepper
1/4 teaspoon finely chopped garlic
1/4 cup clam juice
3 tablespoons coarsely chopped fresh tomato
1 tablespoon Cajun spices
Pinch filé powder
1/4 cup crawfish tails (or chopped, cooked shrimp)
1 tablespoon chopped Italian parsley
Tabasco sauce
Salt and pepper to taste
2 tablespoons clarified butter* or light olive oil
3 eggs
1/4 cup grated cheddar cheese

SMOKED SALMON AND SHIITAKE OMELET

Serves 1 or 2

Here's a tasty, unusual way to use smoked salmon for breakfast. Chives and sour cream freshen up this omelet and balance the smokiness of the salmon and the earthiness of the mushrooms. (You don't always need cheese to make an omelet rich and filling.) Round out the dish with a side of sliced vine-ripened tomatoes drizzled with a little vinaigrette, dilled rye toast, and Crispy Potato Hash (recipe, p. 197) for a fantastic brunch.

What You Need

10-inch nonstick frying pan   Mixing bowl   Whisk   Rubber spatula

How to Make

1. Heat the frying pan. Add olive oil, mushrooms, and 1 tablespoon of red onion and sauté* over medium heat for about 2 minutes or until they soften.
2. In the bowl, whisk eggs with salt and pepper and add to the pan.
3. With the spatula, fluff the omelet,* check to see if it's sticking, and then flip.
4. Sprinkle red onion and chives on the omelet; then lay salmon slices evenly across the top.
5. Spread a little sour cream down the middle and then fold omelet onto a plate.
6. Garnish with a dollop of sour cream and chive sprigs on top.

*See "chop," "dice," and "sauté" in the Glossary; for fluffing an omelet, see Tips and Techniques.

Ingredients

2 tablespoons olive oil
1/4 cup thinly sliced shiitake
    mushrooms
2 tablespoons finely diced* red
    onion
3 eggs
Salt and pepper to taste
1 tablespoon chopped* chives
    plus more for garnish
2 to 3 slices smoked salmon
2 tablespoons sour cream

SPINACH AND GOAT CHEESE OMELET

Makes 1 omelet

When you combine the delicate, creamy flavor of goat cheese, buttery egg, bright fresh spinach, and red tomato, you get the Italian flag in omelet form. You also get a luscious, unusually tangy omelet that has enough character to make a tasty breakfast, lunch, or simple dinner. Serve with Crispy Potato Hash (recipe, p. 197).

What You Need

10-inch nonstick frying pan   Mixing bowl   Whisk   Rubber spatula

How to Make

1. Whisk eggs in the bowl and set aside.
2. Heat the frying pan.
3. Add oil and shallots. Cook for a minute; then add the spinach. Season with a little salt and pepper.
4. When spinach is hot and starting to wilt, add eggs.
5. Using the rubber spatula, fluff the omelet.* Flip and then add Roasted Tomatoes and goat cheese and season with a little more salt and pepper.
6. Fold the omelet onto a plate.

*See "chop" in the Glossary; for blanching and fluffing an omelet, see Tips and Techniques.

Ingredients

2 tablespoons olive oil
1 tablespoon chopped* shallots
1/2 cup fresh spinach, blanched,* water squeezed out, and chopped
Salt and pepper
3 extra-large eggs, whipped
2 halves Roasted Tomatoes, chopped (recipe, p. 204)
3 tablespoons mild goat cheese

ZUCCHINI AND CORN OMELET

Serves 1 or 2

Some omelets — such as this one — are pure summertime on a plate. In summer, sweet corn is in season and makes this dish sunny and golden. You can play around with different cheeses, but I think jack and Cotija work best because they are mild and don't overpower the delicate flavors of the corn and zucchini. Serve this omelet with a couple of grilled tortillas and Black Beans (recipe, p. 188).

What You Need

10-inch nonstick frying pan   Mixing bowl   Whisk   Rubber spatula

How to Make

1. Heat the frying pan over medium heat.
2. Add oil, onions, zucchini, salt, and pepper. Cook until the vegetables are soft but still colorful, about 4 minutes.
3. In the bowl, whisk eggs with a pinch of ancho chile powder and then add to the pan, mixing everything well.
4. With the rubber spatula, fluff the omelet,* cook for another 2 to 3 minutes, and then flip. Sprinkle cheeses on omelet and let cook for 30 seconds.
5. Fold the omelet onto a plate and garnish with Salsa Fresca.

*See "dice" in the Glossary; for fluffing an omelet, see Tips and Techniques.

Ingredients

2 tablespoons olive oil
2 tablespoons finely diced* yellow onion
1/3 cup thinly sliced rounds of zucchini
Salt and pepper to taste
3 extra-large eggs
Ancho chile powder
1/2 cup sweet white corn kernels, cut from the cob
1/4 cup jack cheese
1 tablespoon crumbled Cotija cheese
2 tablespoons Salsa Fresca (recipe, p. 239)

BASIC CREPES

Serves 4 to 6

Making crepes is surprisingly easy, and they're so good because there are so many creative ways to prepare them — sweet or savory, for breakfast, brunch, or dessert. For example, make quick, elegant desserts like crepes Suzettes with Grand Marnier, sweet butter, and a touch of marmalade, or roll up fresh strawberries and whipped cream in a piping hot crepe. Maybe you'll be inspired and create more ambitious crepes with ratatouille and provolone or smoked chicken, asparagus, and morels with a brandied cream sauce.

A cast iron crepe pan or round griddle is a good basic tool, but a 12- or 14-inch nonstick frying pan will work, too. At first, flipping crepes is tricky, but it gets easier with practice.

What You Need

Mixing bowl   Whisk   Crepe spatula or small heat-resistant rubber spatula
Round crepe pan, cast iron griddle, or large low-sided nonstick frying pan
4-ounce ladle   Sheet pan lined with wax paper

Ingredients

2 cups white, all-purpose flour (for whole wheat crepes, substitute 1 cup whole wheat flour for 1 cup white flour)
5 large eggs
3-1/2 cups milk
2 tablespoons melted unsalted butter
Pinch salt
2 tablespoons granulated sugar
1/4 cup clarified butter*
PAM cooking spray*

How to Make

1. In the bowl, whisk together all ingredients except clarified butter. The batter should have a smooth, creamlike consistency.
2. Let batter stand at room temperature for at least 30 minutes.
3. Heat the crepe pan over medium-high heat and rub on clarified butter with a paper towel, covering the pan to the edges. Spray with a little PAM cooking spray to ensure an easy release.
4. With the ladle, pour batter into the pan, rotating the pan with a swirling, circular motion to spread the batter evenly and thinly.
5. Let cook until the top begins to bubble and look dry and the edges are slightly brown.
6. Lift one edge of the crepe with the spatula and flip it over in one sweeping motion, so it lies flat in the pan.
7. Let the other side cook for just a few more seconds; then remove the crepe and set on the sheet pan to cool.
8. Repeat to make the rest of the crepes. Be sure not to stack the hot crepes or they may stick. Cool and then stack with a piece of wax paper between them.
9. Refrigerate, covered so they won't dry out, until ready to use.

*See "PAM cooking spray" in the Glossary; for clarified butter, see Tips and Techniques.

CREPES WITH BROCCOLI, GRUYÈRE, HAM, AND EGG

Makes 4 12-inch prepared crepes

Here's a sumptuous, quick brunch dish. Serve it with Roasted Tomatoes (recipe, p. 204), mixed greens with a light vinaigrette, and ripe melon with a squeeze of lemon and chiffonade* of fresh mint.

What You Need

12-inch nonstick frying pan   Crepe pan or griddle   Mixing bowl   Whisk
4-ounce ladle

Ingredients

1 batch prepared Basic Crepes (recipe, p. 32)
2 tablespoons butter
1/4 cup finely diced* yellow onion
1/2 cup diced honey-baked ham
6 eggs
1/4 cup heavy cream
1 cup blanched* broccoli, chopped*
1 cup shredded Gruyère
1/4 cup clarified butter*
4 tablespoons finely chopped chives

How to Make

1. Prepare Basic Crepes and keep warm in a 200F oven.
2. In the frying pan, add butter and onions. Cook over medium-high heat until onions are translucent, about 3 minutes.
3. Add ham to onions and cook until ham is lightly browned, about 2 more minutes.
4. Crack eggs into the bowl, add cream, and whisk.
5. Add eggs to the pan and begin to scramble with ham and onions.
6. When eggs are halfway cooked, add the broccoli. (Adding the broccoli late in the cooking process helps retain its bright green color.)
7. Cook the eggs easy — that means slightly runny — about 3 to 4 minutes.
8. When eggs are almost ready, add half the Gruyère. Put the cooked egg mixture into a bowl and set aside.
9. Heat the griddle. Rub on a little clarified butter and lay down 1 prepared crepe.
10. Flip over; then sprinkle a little cheese on the crepe and put one-fourth of the egg mixture on one corner of the crepe.
11. Fold the crepe in half over the egg and cheese and then fold in half again.
12. Cook for about 1 minute over medium-high heat; then flip and cook the other side. The crepe should be slightly crisp.
13. Remove the filled crepe to a plate and repeat until all crepes are filled and cooked. Garnish with chives and serve immediately.

*See "chiffonade," "chop," and "dice" in the Glossary; for blanching and clarified butter, see Tips and Techniques.

CHILAQUILES

Makes 1 large or 2 small servings

I love this Mexican-inspired dish that my mother prepared often when I was a child. Traditionally, it's a sort of scramble based on crispy fried tortillas, tomatoes, onions, eggs, queso fresco, crushed dried ancho chiles, and pasilla chiles. My version is a frittata-style adaptation that adds chorizo, sour cream for a topping, and a side of Chipotle Salsa.

This dish is particularly festive, so it's fun to serve for guests. You can make single-size portions, as in this recipe, or increase the amounts accordingly and use a larger pan for a family or party presentation. The recipe specifies chorizo, but shredded chicken or chopped prawns may be used as well.

What You Need

10-inch nonstick frying pan   Mixing bowl   Whisk

How to Make

Preheat oven to 375F.

1. Heat the frying pan over medium-high heat. Add oil and fry* tortilla squares until crispy, about 4 to 5 minutes. Remove from pan and set aside on a towel.
2. Add chorizo and cook until it's lightly browned, about 3 minutes.
3. Add onion and tomato and cook until chorizo is done, about 3 more minutes. Add the fried tortilla squares to this mixture.
4. In the bowl, thoroughly whisk eggs and add to the pan.
5. Add ancho chile powder and a pinch of cumin and stir eggs, chorizo, and tortilla squares together until eggs begin to firm, 2 to 3 minutes.
6. Top with cheeses; then put pan into the oven and bake until mixture is firm, about 4 more minutes.
7. Serve straight from the pan, garnished with sour cream and Salsa Fresca, Roasted Jalapeño, cilantro sprigs, and a side of Chipotle Salsa.

*See "dice" in the Glossary; for frying, see Tips and Techniques.

Ingredients

3 tablespoons canola oil
2 standard-size corn tortillas, cut in 1-1/2-inch squares
4 ounces chorizo sausage
1/4 cup yellow onion, diced*
1/2 tomato, diced
3 eggs
1/2 teaspoon ancho chile powder
Ground cumin
2 tablespoons shredded cheddar cheese
2 tablespoons shredded jack cheese
2 tablespoons queso fresco (available at Mexican markets)
1 tablespoon sour cream
1 tablespoon Salsa Fresca (recipe, p. 239)
1 Roasted Jalapeño (recipe, p. 203)
Cilantro sprigs
2 ounces Chipotle Salsa (recipe, p. 238)

EGGS BENEDICT

Serves 5

This is such a classic, easy dish, yet so many people have told me it's too difficult or would take too long to make. With this simple recipe, you'll be able to spoil your friends and family with beautiful classic brunches. I like to serve eggs Benedict with a side of Crispy Potato Hash (recipe, p. 197), sliced fresh fruit, and berries.

What You Need

2 12-inch nonstick frying pans   Slotted spoon

How to Make

1. Fill a frying pan half full of water and bring water almost to a boil over medium-high heat.
2. Add vinegar; then crack eggs and gently slip them into the water.
3. Poach* for about 3 minutes or longer if you like them cooked more. (The vinegar helps the eggs clump together to form perfect little poached eggs. Be sure not to let the water come to a boil, or it will become very cloudy and the eggs will come apart and be hard to work with.)
4. In the other frying pan, heat a little butter over medium-high heat and brown the Canadian bacon. At the same time, toast the muffins.
5. Place toasted muffins on plates; then lay a slice of Canadian bacon on top of each half.
6. The eggs should be done by now. With a slotted spoon, carefully lift out each egg and place it on a muffin half.
7. Spoon 2 tablespoons of Basic Hollandaise (or more if you like) on each egg and garnish with freshy snipped chives (if using). Serve immediately.

*For poaching, see Tips and Techniques.

Ingredients

10 extra-large eggs
1 tablespoon rice vinegar
Butter or canola oil
10 1/4-inch-thick slices Canadian bacon (or honey-baked ham)
5 English muffins, split
Basic Hollandaise (recipe, p. 230)
Chives (optional)

SMOKED SALMON BENEDICT

Serves 4

There are as many variations on Benedict-style egg dishes as there are popular tunes in the music world. This is one of the most delicious, and after you've made some of the other recipes, it will be a cinch. Crispy Potato Hash (recipe, p. 197) would team perfectly with this dish for Sunday brunch, and a glass of Prosecco or a mimosa or two wouldn't hurt either.

What You Need

12-inch frying pan   Slotted spoon

How to Make

1. Fill the frying pan half full of water and bring water almost to a boil over medium heat.
2. Add vinegar and then crack in the eggs and poach.*
3. Toast the muffins.
4. To the Basic Hollandaise, add dill.
5. Place toasted muffins on plates and top each half with a tomato slice and a slice of salmon.
6. Eggs should be done after about 3 minutes; cook a minute more if you prefer firmer eggs. Remove with the slotted spoon and place on top of the salmon. Top with 2 tablespoons of dill hollandaise and a little red onion. Serve immediately.

*See "chop" and "dice" in the Glossary; for poaching, see Tips and Techniques.

Ingredients

1 tablespoon rice vinegar
8 eggs
4 English muffins, split
Basic Hollandaise (recipe, p. 230)
1/4 cup chopped* fresh dill
8 slices ripe tomato
8 slices smoked salmon
1/4 cup finely diced* red onion

MEXICAN BENEDICT

Serves 4

Talk about a crowd-pleaser — the Mexican Benedict is one of the most popular brunch dishes at our restaurants. Part of its charm is the multicultural flavor of chorizo and avocado combined with poached egg and hollandaise sauce and the folded tortilla that replaces the English muffin. Serve it with a side of Black Beans (recipe, p. 188) and sliced papaya or mango or with Crispy Potato Hash (recipe, p. 197) and fruit.

What You Need

12-inch frying pan   10-inch nonstick frying pan   Slotted spoon

How to Make

Preheat oven to 400F.

1. Fill the 10-inch nonstick frying pan half full of water and bring water almost to a boil over medium-high heat.
2. Add vinegar to water, crack eggs, and gently slide them into the pan. Poach* for about 3 to 4 minutes, depending on how soft you like them.
3. Place tortillas in the preheated oven.
4. In the 12-inch frying pan, fry* the chorizo patties until fully cooked.
5. Take the tortillas out of the oven and fold into quarters, placing two on each plate.
6. Pat the chorizo patties dry on paper towels and then place one on each folded tortilla.
7. Cut avocados into quarters, slice each quarter, and fan slices from one quarter across each patty.
8. By now, the eggs should be done. Using a slotted spoon, carefully remove them from the pan and place one on top of each avocado and chorizo stack.
9. Finish each stack by smoothing 2 tablespoons of Basic Hollandaise on the egg and top with 1 tablespoon of Salsa Fresca. Garnish with cilantro sprigs. Serve immediately.

*For frying and poaching, see Tips and Techniques.

Ingredients

1 tablespoon rice vinegar
8 eggs
8 corn tortillas
8 chorizo patties, 2 ounces each
2 avocados
Basic Hollandaise (recipe, p. 230)
1/2 cup Salsa Fresca (recipe, p. 239)
Cilantro sprigs

ROASTED CHICKEN HASH

Serves 4

Traditionally, hashes were made with leftovers, particularly from large meals featuring big joints of meat such as corned beef, roast beef, or turkey. For this dish, we roast a chicken just to make the hash and use the pan drippings to make the gravy. You can do all of that the night before.

This hash is sure to please your family, especially on a cold, rainy morning. Fresh-baked Buttermilk Biscuits (recipe, p. 182) go best with this dish.

What You Need

9 x 13-inch roasting pan   Sheet pan   Clear glass cup or bowl for drippings
12-inch frying pan   10-inch nonstick frying pan   Gravy dish or bowl

How to Make

FOR THE CHICKEN AND GRAVY:

Preheat oven to 375F.

1. Wash the chicken thoroughly; then rub with olive oil. Salt and pepper well, inside and out.
2. Place chicken in the roasting pan. Do not line the pan with foil because you will need all the caramelized drippings to make the gravy.
3. Roast chicken for about 1 hour and 15 minutes.
4. Remove from the oven and let rest for 30 minutes.
5. Take chicken out of the pan and set on a large sheet pan. Pour drippings from the roasting pan into a clear glass cup or bowl.
6. Put the roasting pan on a burner and add chicken stock. Skim the fat off the top of the drippings, leaving only the natural juice, and add the drippings to the pan. Whisk together until well combined.
7. Whisk the water and flour together and add to the simmering stock and drippings. Continue whisking and scraping the bottom of the pan until the gravy begins to thicken.
8. Whisk in butter.
9. Add thyme and then salt and pepper to taste.
10. Pour gravy into a gravy dish or bowl and set aside.
11. When the chicken is cool enough to handle, remove the skin and shred the meat by hand. Make sure there are no bones. Save the carcass for stock.

Ingredients

For the chicken and gravy
(makes about 1-1/2 cups):

1 3-pound roasting chicken
2 tablespoons olive oil
Salt and pepper
1-1/2 cups chicken stock
1/4 cup water
3 tablespoons all-purpose flour
1 tablespoon unsalted butter
1/2 teaspoon chopped* fresh thyme

FOR THE HASH:

1. In the 12-inch frying pan heated to medium-high, add olive oil and butter.
2. Add potatoes and cook over medium-high heat until golden brown and crispy, about 10 minutes.
3. Add onions and peppers and cook until soft, another 4 minutes.
4. Add chicken meat, artichoke hearts, and a pinch of cayenne. Stir together well and then let sit for a while without stirring, to let the hash brown and caramelize. Then stir a little more.
5. When the hash looks browned and caramelized, add the spinach, half the parsley, and salt and pepper to taste. Cook for a couple more minutes and then divide among four plates.
6. In the 10-inch frying pan, cook eggs any style. Top the hash on each plate with 2 eggs; then spoon on a little gravy and finish with a little more chopped parsley. Serve immediately.

*See "chop" and "dice" in the Glossary; for blanching, see Tips and Techniques.

Ingredients continued

For the hash:

2 tablespoons olive oil
1 tablespoon unsalted butter
1-1/2 cups cooked, diced* russet
    potatoes
1/2 cup diced red onion
1/3 cup diced red bell pepper
Shredded roasted chicken
1/2 cup chopped artichoke
    hearts, cooked fresh or
    canned in brine
Cayenne pepper
1/2 cup chopped blanched*
    spinach
1/4 cup chopped Italian parsley
Salt and pepper
8 extra-large eggs
Roasted chicken gravy

DEEP-DISH FRITTATA

Serves 8

This dish is so simple yet turns out beautifully with its colorful layers of vegetables and meats. Frittata does take a little longer than an omelet to prep and bake, but cutting into those thick lasagna-like slices makes it all worthwhile.

You could cook this the day before you plan to serve it; then reheat the pieces or even serve chilled for a picnic. It's delicious hot or cold. Feel free to try different ingredients. Play around. A side salad of tossed greens is the perfect accompaniment.

What You Need

12-inch nonstick frying pan   Large mixing bowl   Whisk   Cookie sheet
9 x 13-inch glass baking dish

How to Make

Preheat oven to 375F.

1. In the frying pan, add olive oil and sauté* bacon and sausage over medium-high heat for 6 to 8 minutes.
2. Add onions, cook 4 minutes more, and then add mushrooms, zucchini, broccoli, potato, spinach, tomato, and basil. Add a little salt and pepper to taste.
3. Cook until ingredients soften slightly and sweat,* about 4 more minutes. Remove from heat.
4. In the bowl, crack the eggs and whisk together with cream.
5. Fold in the meat-and-vegetable mixture. Season with more salt and pepper to taste.
6. Pour into the baking dish. The egg mixture should be about 2 inches deep with at least an extra inch of space at the top.
7. Sprinkle the mozzarella and Parmesan on top.
8. Set baking dish on top of a cookie sheet and bake for about 1 hour or until the center of the frittata is firm. Let cool about 15 minutes before cutting.

* See "chop," "dice," "Parmesan," "sauté," and "sweat" in the Glossary; for blanching, see Tips and Techniques.

Ingredients

3 tablespoons olive oil
6 slices bacon, chopped
1/2 cup diced* Italian sausage
1 small yellow onion, diced
1/2 cup sliced mushrooms
1/2 cup diced zucchini
1 cup chopped,* blanched* broccoli
1/2 cup cooked, diced potato
1 cup chopped, blanched spinach
1/2 cup diced fresh tomato
1/4 cup chopped fresh basil
Salt and pepper
15 large eggs
1/2 cup heavy cream
1/2 cup grated mozzarella
1/4 cup grated Parmesan*

FRITTATA WITH ASPARAGUS, FONTINA, AND PESTO

Serves 4

This frittata whips up much more quickly than the Deep-Dish Frittata on page 43. In fact, it's a bit like a pizza. You can slice it into pie-shaped wedges, or make it in smaller pans for individual servings. If you have a hard time finding fontina cheese, a Gruyère or Swiss cheese would substitute perfectly. Pair this with a crisp green salad or fresh fruit medley.

What You Need

Large mixing bowl   Rubber spatula or wooden spoon
12-inch frying pan, one that can go from stovetop to oven

How to Make

Preheat oven to 375F.

1. Chop the asparagus stalks into small pieces about 1-1/2 inches long. Save the tips and set aside.
2. In the bowl, whisk the eggs with the cream and Pesto.
3. Heat the frying pan over medium-high heat. Add the olive oil; then add the onions and a pinch of salt and pepper and cook until soft, about 4 minutes.
4. Add the chopped asparagus and cook for a couple of seconds; then add the egg mixture.
5. Lower heat to medium. With a rubber spatula, stir the eggs, making sure to scrape the bottom and edges of the pan.
6. As eggs start to get a little firm, top with asparagus tips, fontina, Grana Padano, pine nuts, and Roasted Tomatoes. Make sure you distribute all these ingredients evenly on the frittata.
7. Place pan in oven and bake for 8 to 10 minutes or until cheese is lightly browned and eggs are firm. Serve hot or cold.

*See "dice," "Grana Padano," and "Parmesan" in the Glossary; for blanching and toasting, see Tips and Techniques.

Ingredients

1 bunch (about 1-1/2 pounds) fresh asparagus, blanched*
8 extra-large eggs
1/4 cup heavy cream
2 tablespoons Pesto (recipe, p. 235)
3 tablespoons olive oil
1/4 cup finely diced* yellow onion
Salt and pepper
1/2 cup shredded fontina cheese
2 tablespoons grated Grana Padano* or Parmesan*
3 tablespoons toasted* pine nuts
6 halves Roasted Tomatoes, (recipe, p. 204)

BURGERS
AND
SANDWICHES

BURGERS AND SANDWICHES

I love a great sandwich for lunch or dinner because, hot or cold, sandwiches are substantial and satisfying. There's no end to what you can put inside a bun or between two slices of bread, from leftover meatloaf to grilled beef medallions or fresh salmon. The most important ingredient in building a sandwich is the bread. Quite simply, if you have really good bread, you will have a great sandwich.

GRILLED LAMB SANDWICHES

Makes 4 sandwiches

For this sandwich, I use lamb sirloin tips seasoned with a simple marinade. Lamb loin could be used as well, but it's more expensive. The thin slices of lamb combine with the distinctive tastes of watercress, red onion, and Roasted Tomatoes, all enlivened with a little rosemary aioli that really makes this sandwich shine.

What You Need

Container   Mixing bowl   Grill   Whisk

How to Make

FOR THE LAMB:

1. In the container, combine all ingredients.
2. Cover and let lamb marinate overnight in the refrigerator.

FOR THE ROSEMARY AIOLI:

In the bowl, whisk all ingredients together. Set aside.

FOR THE SANDWICHES:

1. Grill* the meat over medium-high heat until it's medium-rare, about 4 to 5 minutes per side, and set aside to rest.
2. Split and toast the buns.
3. Spread the bottom half of each bun with a little rosemary aioli and place some watercress on top.
4. Slice lamb thinly across the grain and place on top of the watercress.
5. Layer a slice of red onion and a Roasted Tomato half, add a little more rosemary aioli, and cover with the top half of the bun. Serve immediately.

*See "chop" in the Glossary; for grilling, see Tips and Techniques.

Ingredients

For the lamb:

4 5-ounce pieces of lamb
    sirloin tips
2 tablespoons chopped* fresh
    rosemary, stems removed
2 tablespoons chopped garlic
2 tablespoons Worcestershire
    sauce
3 tablespoons olive oil
1 tablespoon Dijon mustard

For the rosemary aioli:

1/2 cup mayonnaise
1-1/2 tablespoons lemon juice
1 tablespoon Worcestershire
    sauce
1 tablespoon Dijon mustard
1 tablespoon chopped garlic
1 tablespoon chopped fresh
    rosemary, stems removed
Shot of Tabasco sauce

For the sandwiches:

Marinated lamb
4 rosemary buns
1/2 cup rosemary aioli
4 halves Roasted Tomatoes
    (recipe, p. 204)
4 thin slices red onion
1 bunch upland watercress

GRILLED AHI SANDWICHES

Serves 4

Ginger-cucumber relish and wasabi aioli bring this sandwich to life. A favorite in our restaurants, it's an easy way to impress your friends and family. I like to pair it with a basic green salad dressed with ginger vinaigrette (see Chinese Almond Chicken Salad, p. 100).

What You Need

2 small mixing bowls   Whisk   Cast iron grill or frying pan

How to Make

FOR THE WASABI AIOLI:

In a bowl, combine all ingredients and mix well with a whisk. Set aside.

FOR THE GINGER-CUCUMBER RELISH:

In a bowl, combine all ingredients and mix well. Set aside.

FOR THE SANDWICHES:

1. Salt and pepper the ahi tuna and grill* or pan-sear over high heat to medium-rare, about 2 to 2-1/2 minutes per side. The edges should be browned, but the interior should still be rosy.
2. Split and toast the buns.
3. Spread a little aioli on the bottom half of each bun and then layer on the sprouts, sliced tomato, sliced red onion, grilled ahi, one-quarter of the sliced avocado, and the ginger-cucumber relish.
4. Dab a little aioli on the underside of the top half of each bun, place on the sandwich, and cut sandwich in half diagonally to display the pretty layers.

*See "chop" and "dice" in the Glossary; for grilling, see Tips and Techniques.

Ingredients

For the wasabi aioli:

1/3 cup mayonnaise
3 tablespoons wasabi paste
2 tablespoons rice vinegar

For the ginger-cucumber relish:

1 cup peeled, seeded, and
    diced* cucumber
1/4 cup finely diced red onion
1/4 cup chopped* green onion,
    green and white parts
1/4 cup chopped pickled ginger
2 tablespoons rice vinegar
1/4 cup chopped cilantro
1 tablespoon granulated sugar
Salt and pepper to taste

For the sandwiches:

4 4-1/2-ounce ahi tuna steaks,
    cut about 1/2 inch thick
Salt and pepper to taste
4 ciabatta buns
4 tablespoons wasabi aioli
1 cup alfalfa sprouts
8 thin slices tomato
4 1/4-inch-thick slices red onion
1 avocado, sliced in lengthwise
    strips
1 cup ginger-cucumber relish

BARBECUED PULLED PORK SANDWICHES

Makes 13 to 16 sandwiches

Hot from the oven, juicy and tender, these fragrant pork pillows are definitely a treat. There's some extra prep time involved for the meat, but overall they're easy to make. You do need a smoker or at least a barbecue with a lid so you can seal in the smoke from the wood chips. If you can't smoke the meat, substitute liquid smoke, but use it sparingly and only as a last resort. Top this sandwich with a little Memphis Coleslaw for a slightly spicy, refreshing crunch and serve with Creole Potato Salad (recipe, p. 192).

What You Need

Smoker or barbecue with lid
Large, ovenproof braising pot
1 pound soaked applewood chips

How to Make

FOR THE PORK:

Preheat oven to 400F.

1. Mix the dry ingredients together and rub generously all over the pork. Cover pork with plastic wrap and let sit for a few hours in the refrigerator.
2. While the pork is resting in its rub, put the wood chips in the smoker and start it up at low heat. Unwrap the pork, set it in the smoker, and cover with the lid. Watch to make sure the wood chips release smoke continuously for about 1 hour.
3. On the bottom of the braising pot, place the onions and garlic. Remove the pork from the smoker and place it on top of the onions and garlic. Pour beer over the pork, cover, and set in the oven for about 2-1/2 to 3 hours or until the meat falls apart at the touch.
4. Take the pork out of the oven and let cool for 15 to 20 minutes; then shred the meat off the bone, removing and discarding the fat.
5. Toss the pork with the barbecue sauce.

FOR THE SANDWICHES:

1. Split and toast the buns.
2. Pile shredded pork on the bottom half of each bun, top with a little Memphis Coleslaw, and cover with the top half of the bun. Enjoy with an ice-cold Anchor Steam.

*See "chop" and "smash" in the Glossary.

Ingredients

For the pork:

1 10-pound pork butt, bone in, cut into 4 pieces
1 teaspoon cayenne pepper
3 tablespoons paprika
3 tablespoons chili powder
1 tablespoon ground cumin
1 teaspoon cinnamon
3 tablespoons garlic powder
3 tablespoons onion powder
4 tablespoons brown sugar
1 tablespoon dried thyme
2 tablespoons curry powder
4 tablespoons salt
2 tablespoons ground black pepper
2 bottles Anchor Steam beer or ale
2 medium yellow onions, chopped*
7 cloves garlic, peeled and smashed*
1-1/2 cups of your favorite barbecue sauce

For the sandwiches:

Barbecued pulled pork
16 good-quality burger buns
2 cups Memphis Coleslaw (recipe, p. 187)

GRILLED TRI-TIP SANDWICHES

Serves 6

This is one robust steak sandwich. I use tri-tip because it's so tender when sliced thinly across the grain. Caramelized Onions add juicy sweetness, horseradish aioli contributes some spice, and a bit of blue cheese takes this sandwich to the next level of sophistication. Try it with Citrus Fingerling Potato Salad (recipe, p. 193), Fried Onions (recipe, p. 226), and Anchor Steam beer. This tri-tip also makes an appealing main dish. Serve with Mashed Potatoes (recipe, p. 191), grilled asparagus, salsa, and Fried Onions.

What You Need

Mixing bowl   Container   8-inch sauté pan   Grill   Meat thermometer
Wire rack

How to Make

FOR THE TRI-TIP:

1. Combine all marinade ingredients.
2. Rub meat well with the marinade. Place in container, cover, and let sit in the refrigerator for at least 2 hours or, even better, overnight.

FOR THE HORSERADISH AIOLI:

In the bowl, mix all ingredients together well. Set aside.

Ingredients

For the tri-tip:

2 1-1/2-pound tri-tips, trimmed
1/4 cup ketchup
2 tablespoons cider vinegar
3 tablespoons brown sugar
3 tablespoons light soy sauce
2 tablespoons chopped* garlic
3 shallots, chopped
2 tablespoons chopped fresh thyme
2 tablespoons chopped fresh rosemary
Pinch cayenne pepper
1 tablespoon Tabasco sauce
2 tablespoons Worcestershire sauce
2 bay leaves
3 tablespoons olive oil
Salt and pepper to taste

For the horseradish aioli:

1 cup mayonnaise
3 tablespoons prepared white horseradish
2 tablespoons lemon juice
1/2 teaspoon chopped garlic
Salt and pepper to taste

FOR THE SANDWICHES:

1. Prepare the grill to medium heat. (The temperature is key. If the heat is too high, the meat will burn; if it's too low, the meat will take forever to cook.) Scrape off excess marinade; then salt and pepper the meat on both sides.

2. Grill* tri-tips for 5 minutes on one side. Then flip over and grill for another 5 minutes. Flip back to the first side, making sure the grill marks cross, and grill for 5 more minutes. Flip again, setting down so the grill marks cross, and grill for 5 more minutes. If the temperature on your grill is right, this should bring the meat to medium-rare. Insert a meat thermometer into the thickest part of the tri-tip; it should read 110–115F for a great medium-rare.

3. Pull meat off the grill and let rest on a wire rack for at least 15 minutes.

4. Find the grain of the meat and cut thin slices against the grain. This ensures tenderness.

5. Cut baguette into 6-inch lengths. Then slice each length in half and pull out some of the soft bread inside. Heat the bread on the grill or in the oven.

6. In the sauté pan, warm up the Caramelized Onions.

7. Spread a little horseradish aioli on the bread; then top with some watercress and a generous amount of meat, about 6 to 8 ounces per sandwich.

8. Salt and pepper the meat and then add blue cheese and Caramelized Onions to your taste. Serve right away.

*See "chop" in the Glossary; for grilling, see Tips and Techniques.

Ingredients continued

For the sandwiches:
Marinated tri-tip
Salt and pepper to taste
Fresh baguette
1 cup Caramelized Onions
 (recipe, p. 223)
1/2 cup horseradish aioli
1 bunch watercress
1/2 cup crumbled blue cheese
 of your choice

GRILLED MAHI MAHI SANDWICHES

Makes 4 sandwiches

This Hawaii-inspired summertime sandwich is perfect for cooking up at a barbecue, whether it's at the beach or in your backyard. It features grilled marinated mahi mahi, a tropical fruit salsa, and ginger aioli. The flavors are fresh and exciting. Serve with Asian Soba Noodle Salad (recipe, p. 190) for a complete lunch.

What You Need

Container   Food processor   Mixing bowl   Grill

How to Make

FOR THE MAHI MAHI:

In the container, combine all ingredients, cover, and marinate fish for at least 2 hours in the refrigerator.

FOR THE TROPICAL FRUIT SALSA:

In the bowl, mix all ingredients together and let stand for 1 hour.

FOR THE GINGER AIOLI:

1. In the food processor, add mayonnaise, fresh ginger, green onions, cilantro, and pickled ginger and purée well.
2. Add a little salt and pepper to taste.

FOR THE SANDWICHES:

1. Grill* mahi mahi over medium-high heat so the outside is seared but the interior is still juicy, about 4 to 4-1/2 minutes on each side.
2. Split and toast the buns and place a little aioli and lettuce on the bottom half of each one.
3. Place a piece of fish on top of the lettuce.
4. Spoon a little fruit salsa and ginger aioli onto the fish and cover with the top half of the bun. Serve immediately.

*See "chop" and "dice" in the Glossary; for grilling, see Tips and Techniques.

Ingredients

For the mahi mahi:

4 4-1/2-ounce mahi mahi fillets
1 tablespoon sesame oil
1/4 cup chopped* green onions, white and green parts
1 tablespoon chopped fresh ginger
2 tablespoons canola oil

For the tropical fruit salsa:

1/2 cup diced* ripe papaya
1/2 cup diced ripe mango
1/2 cup diced ripe pineapple
2 finely diced red Fresno chiles
1/4 cup chopped green onions, white and green parts
1/4 cup chopped cilantro
1/4 cup diced red onion
1 tablespoon sesame oil
1 tablespoon granulated sugar
3 tablespoons lime juice
1 tablespoon black sesame seeds
Salt and pepper to taste

Ingredients continued

For the ginger aioli:

1 cup mayonnaise
1 tablespoon chopped fresh
   ginger
3 tablespoons chopped green
   onions, white and green parts
3 tablespoons chopped cilantro
1 ounce pickled ginger, chopped
Salt and pepper

For the sandwiches:

4 pieces marinated mahi mahi
4 buns
1 cup shredded romaine lettuce
4 tablespoons ginger aioli
1 cup tropical fruit salsa

FRIED CATFISH SANDWICHES

Serves 4

This great fish sandwich — seasoned with Cajun spices, fried crisp, and topped with a little rémoulade — will make you think you're sitting next to a bayou in Louisiana. Serve with a side of Memphis Coleslaw (recipe, p. 187).

What You Need

Bowl   Plate   Sheet pan   12-inch deep-sided frying pan   Wire rack

How to Make

FOR THE SEASONED FLOUR:

Mix all ingredients together and set aside.

FOR THE CATFISH:

1. In the bowl, marinate the catfish with the buttermilk, garlic, a pinch of salt, and a pinch of pepper for at least a couple of hours in the refrigerator.
2. Place some of the seasoned flour on a plate and coat the fish generously with the flour. Set the coated fish on a sheet pan to rest for at least 15 minutes.
3. In the frying pan, heat the Crisco over medium heat; the fat should be about 3/4 of an inch deep.
4. When the Crisco is hot but not smoking, lay in the catfish two pieces at a time. (This makes it easier to work with.)
5. Fry* until fish is golden brown and crispy on one side, about 4 minutes. Flip the pieces over and fry the other side for another 4 minutes.
6. Remove catfish from the pan and set on the wire rack to drain.

FOR THE SANDWICHES:

1. Split and toast the buns.
2. On the bottom half of each bun, layer chopped lettuce, sliced tomato, sliced onion, and fried catfish. Top with a little rémoulade and cover with the top half of the bun. Serve hot.

*See "smash" in the Glossary; for frying, see Tips and Techniques.

Ingredients

For the seasoned flour:

1-1/2 cups all-purpose flour
4 tablespoons garlic powder
4 tablespoons onion powder
1/2 cup fine cornmeal or semolina
1/3 teaspoon cayenne pepper
1/3 teaspoon dried thyme
1/2 teaspoon paprika
1/3 teaspoon baking powder
2 tablespoons salt
1/2 teaspoon freshly ground black pepper

For the catfish:

4 4-ounce pieces cleaned catfish
1 cup buttermilk
3 garlic cloves, peeled and smashed*
Salt and freshly ground black pepper
Seasoned flour
1-1/2 cups Crisco

For the sandwiches:

4 ciabatta buns or hoagie rolls
1/2 cup rémoulade (see Prawn and Peperonata Sandwiches, p. 62)
1-1/2 cups shredded iceberg or romaine lettuce
2 ripe tomatoes, sliced
4 thin slices red onion

BRAISED BRISKET SANDWICHES

Serves 4 to 6

Braising this cut of meat with beer, sun-dried tomatoes, onion soup mix, garlic, and herbs gives the beef a beautifully rich flavor. I like to balance it with refreshing Memphis Coleslaw and a topping of crispy Fried Onions. You can cook the meat the day before and reheat it with a little braising liquid when you're ready to serve the sandwiches.

What You Need

Large ovenproof braising pot, such as Le Creuset

How to Make

FOR THE BRISKET:

Preheat oven to 400F.

1. Season the brisket with salt and pepper.
2. In the braising pot, add olive oil and brown the brisket over medium-high heat for 6 to 8 minutes on each side.
3. Deglaze* the pot with the red wine to loosen any browned bits that stick to the pan. Add the vinegar and then the beer.
4. Add beef stock, fresh tomatoes, sun-dried tomatoes, onions, garlic, celery, sugar, herbs, parsley, and onion soup mix.
5. Cover the pot and braise the brisket in the oven for 3-1/2 hours, checking occasionally to see that the liquid hasn't boiled away. If the meat looks dry, add some water and continue cooking. It's done when it starts to fall apart when pierced with a fork.
6. Take the brisket out of the pot and let rest for about 20 minutes. Then slice thinly across the grain.
7. Reduce* braising liquid until it thickens. Set aside.

FOR THE SANDWICHES:

1. Split and toast the onion rolls.
2. Put a little Memphis Coleslaw on the bottom half of each roll. Lay the sliced brisket on the coleslaw and add a little liquid from the pot, a dab of Dijon mustard, and some Fried Onions. Cover with the top half of the roll. Serve with a stout or rich amber ale.

*See "chop," "deglaze," "reduce," and "smash" in the Glossary.

Ingredients

For the brisket:

1 5-pound beef brisket
Salt and pepper to taste
5 tablespoons olive oil
1 cup burgundy wine (of a quality you'd like to drink)
1/4 cup red wine vinegar
1 bottle of your favorite amber ale
2 cups beef stock
1 cup chopped fresh tomatoes
1/2 cup sun-dried tomatoes, finely chopped*
1 yellow onion, finely chopped
6 garlic cloves, peeled and smashed*
1 stalk celery, finely chopped
1/4 cup granulated sugar
2 fresh thyme sprigs
1 fresh rosemary sprig
2 bay leaves
1/3 cup chopped Italian parsley
1 packet Lipton Onion Soup

For the sandwiches:

4 to 6 onion rolls
2 cups Fried Onions (recipe, p. 226)
6 tablespoons Dijon mustard
2 cups Memphis Coleslaw (recipe, p. 187)

CRAB AND HEARTS OF PALM SANDWICHES

Makes 4 sandwiches

This elegant, light sandwich celebrates the sweet flavor of Dungeness crab, and the layers of toasted sourdough bread, sprouts, tomato, dill Havarti, and avocado provide a colorful complement of tastes and textures. Citrus Fingerling Potato Salad (recipe, p. 193) would go beautifully with this sandwich.

What You Need

Mixing bowl

How to Make

FOR THE CRAB SALAD:

1. In the bowl, thoroughly mix together all the ingredients.
2. Season with salt and pepper to taste.

FOR THE SANDWICHES:

1. Lightly toast the sliced sourdough.
2. On a slice of bread, place a slice of Havarti, some alfalfa sprouts, and a layer of sliced tomato, fan avocado slices across the tomatoes, and finish with the crab salad.
3. Top with another slice of bread. (Optional: Omit the second slice of bread and serve as an open-faced sandwich.)
4. Slice the sandwiches in half so the colors are visible.

*See "chop," "dice," and "White Wine Worcestershire Sauce" in the Glossary.

Ingredients

For the crab salad:

2 cups cleaned Dungeness crab meat with extra liquid squeezed out so the meat is dry
1 cup chopped,* well-drained canned hearts of palm
1/3 cup finely diced* red onion
1 celery stalk, finely diced
2 tablespoons chopped fresh dill
1 tablespoon chopped fresh tarragon
2 tablespoons lemon juice
Dash Tabasco sauce
2 tablespoons White Wine Worcestershire Sauce*
1/2 cup mayonnaise
Salt and pepper

For the sandwiches:

8 slices good-quality sourdough bread
4 slices dill Havarti
Alfalfa sprouts
Tomato slices
2 avocados, sliced
Crab salad

PRAWN AND PEPERONATA SANDWICHES

Makes 4 sandwiches

These sandwiches will remind you of a New Orleans–style po' boy. Poached prawns are sliced and tossed with rémoulade and then stuffed into hoagie rolls with roasted marinated peppers and onions. Make sure you use a lot of shrimp — half the fun here is abundance. Serve with Creole Potato Salad (recipe, p. 192).

What You Need

Food processor   Mixing bowl

How to Make

FOR THE RÉMOULADE:

In the food processor, blend all ingredients well. Set aside.

FOR THE PEPERONATA:

In the bowl, combine all ingredients. Set aside.

FOR THE SANDWICHES:

1. Toss the prawns with the rémoulade and then salt and pepper to taste.
2. Line each roll with 1/4 cup lettuce and 2 slices of tomato.
3. Fill with prawns (5 per sandwich) and top each roll with 2 tablespoons of peperonata.

*See "chop," "julienne," and "White Wine Worcestershire Sauce" in the Glossary; for deveining, poaching, and roasting peppers, see Tips and Techniques.

Ingredients

For the rémoulade:

1 cup mayonnaise
2 tablespoons Creole mustard
2 tablespoons dry sherry
1 tablespoon chopped* garlic
2 tablespoons chopped yellow onion
1 tablespoon White Wine Worcestershire Sauce*
1/4 teaspoon cayenne pepper
2 tablespoons lemon juice
2 tablespoons Tabasco sauce

For the peperonata:

2 red bell peppers, roasted,* peeled, seeded, and julienned*
2 yellow bell peppers, roasted, peeled, seeded, and julienned
1 green bell pepper, roasted, peeled, seeded, and julienned
1/2 red onion, sliced thin
2 tablespoons chopped capers
2 tablespoons sherry vinegar
1 tablespoon finely chopped garlic
2 tablespoons chopped Italian parsley
2 tablespoons extra-virgin olive oil
Salt and pepper to taste

Ingredients continued

For the sandwiches:

20 3-inch prawns, peeled,
deveined,* tails removed,
poached* (do not overcook),
and cut lengthwise
8 tablespoons rémoulade
Salt and pepper
4 hoagie rolls
1 cup shredded iceberg lettuce
8 thin slices tomato
8 tablespoons peperonata

GRILLED FONTINA, PROSCIUTTO, AND ASPARAGUS PANINI

Serves 1

This is a rich, panini-style sandwich, grilled until it's piping hot so that the cheese and prosciutto melt together and release their savory aromas. Think of it as an elegant version of a grilled cheese sandwich. I like to serve it with Heirloom Tomato Bread Soup (recipe, p. 78).

What You Need

Griddle or nonstick grill pan   Spatula

How to Make

1. Lightly brush both sides of the bread with olive oil.
2. Place a slice of fontina on each piece of bread.
3. On one half of the bread, place tomato slices, asparagus, basil, and prosciutto.
4. Place the other piece of bread on top.
5. Add olive oil to the griddle. Cook sandwich over medium heat, pressing down on it with a spatula until it's brown and crisp on one side, about 3 minutes.
6. Flip and repeat on the other side. If you have a large griddle, put 2 or more sandwiches on it and press them down by covering them with a grill weight or a clean brick.

*For blanching, see Tips and Techniques.

.

Ingredients

2 slices sourdough bread or ciabatta
2 tablespoons olive oil plus more for brushing
2 slices fontina cheese
2 slices fresh tomato
4 asparagus stalks, peeled and blanched*
3 fresh basil leaves
3 thin slices prosciutto

LAMB BURGERS WITH CUCUMBER-YOGURT SAUCE

Serves 4

If you love lamb, you can't do better than these juicy, aromatic burgers. A little seasoning added to the ground lamb and a quick cucumber-yogurt sauce make for an amazing hot sandwich. For the bread, try rosemary buns. Just be sure the bread isn't too thick or it will mask the subtleties of the lamb. I recommend Crispy French Fries (recipe, p. 198) on the side.

What You Need

Grill   2 mixing bowls

How to Make

FOR THE CUCUMBER-YOGURT SAUCE:

In a bowl, combine ingredients well and set aside.

FOR THE LAMB PATTIES:

1. In a bowl, mix ground lamb with the spices, onions, herbs, Worcestershire sauce, garlic, and a little salt and pepper.
2. Form meat into 8-ounce patties. Pack them well so there are no air pockets; otherwise they'll fall apart.
3. Grill* the patties over medium-high heat to the desired doneness. Medium-rare works best for me (the interiors should be nice and pink), about 4 minutes per side.

FOR THE BURGERS:

1. Split and toast the buns.
2. Quickly grill the onions and heat the Roasted Tomatoes.
3. Brush a little olive oil on the bottom half of each bun and then place some watercress on top.
4. Put a lamb patty on the watercress and follow with a grilled onion, a Roasted Tomato half, and a couple of spoonfuls of the cucumber-yogurt sauce. Cover with the top half of the bun. Serve immediately.

*See "chop" and "dice" in the Glossary; for grilling, see Tips and Techniques.

Ingredients

For the cucumber-yogurt sauce:

1/2 English cucumber, peeled, seeded, and diced*
3/4 cup plain yogurt
1/4 cup sour cream
2 tablespoons lemon juice
1/3 teaspoon ground cumin
1/4 cup chopped* parsley
1/4 chopped fresh mint
Salt and peper to taste

For the lamb patties:

2 pounds ground lamb
2 tablespoons curry powder
1 teaspoon ground cumin
1/2 cup finely chopped yellow onion
1 tablespoon oregano
2 tablespoons chopped fresh mint
2 tablespoons Worcestershire sauce
1 tablespoon chopped garlic
Salt and freshly ground black pepper to taste

For the burgers:

4 rosemary buns
4 medium-thick slices red onion
4 halves Roasted Tomatoes (recipe, p. 204)
Olive oil
1 bunch watercress or 1-1/2 cups baby arugula
Grilled lamb patties
1 cup cucumber-yogurt sauce

SOUPS, STEW, CHILI

SOUPS, STEW, CHILI

There's nothing like a steaming bowl of soup, stew, or chili to warm you up on a cold day. Enjoy it as a light lunch or dinner with grilled cheese sandwiches, cornbread, or hot sourdough.

Cooking soups and stews is one of the oldest methods of preparing food. One-pot meals were simple to make, typically over a fire. And cooking food in large amounts of liquid meant you were able to feed more people with fewer ingredients.

We're lucky. Today, we make soups, stews, and chilis for other reasons, and it just takes imagination and a beautiful selection of fresh ingredients to create something wonderful. Use these recipes to develop your technique. Once you've mastered the basics, the sky's the limit.

CELERY ROOT, APPLE, AND FENNEL SOUP

Serves 4 to 6

Texture is everything in this beautifully creamy soup that's both sweet and savory, and the mint pesto really brings the soup to life. While it's satisfying any time of the year, it's particularly flavorful if you prepare it in the autumn, when the new crop of apples is hitting the stores. Serve it chilled, during the last warm days of early October, or hot, when those biting winds kick in. Either way, it's a pleasure.

What You Need

5-quart stockpot   Hand-held immersion or standing blender

How to Make

FOR THE MINT PESTO:

In the blender, combine all the ingredients into a sauce. Set aside.

FOR THE SOUP:

1. In the stockpot, melt butter over medium-low heat until it begins to lightly brown and then sauté* the celery, apple, celery root, bay leaf, and onion until they're well sweated,* about 4 minutes.
2. Add flour and mix well.
3. Add chicken stock, apple juice, cream, potatoes, sugar, and Roasted Fennel Bulbs and their reserved juices. Bring to a boil; turn down and simmer* over low-medium heat for about 45 minutes.
4. Mix cornstarch with 3 tablespoons of water, blend well, and add to soup. Let simmer for 5 more minutes.
5. Pull off the heat and remove the bay leaf.
6. Purée with a hand-held blender or in small batches with a standing blender. Add salt and pepper to taste.
7. Serve with a drizzle of mint pesto on top.

*See "chop," "dice," "sauté," "simmer," and "sweat" in the Glossary.

Ingredients

For the mint pesto:

1/2 cup fresh mint leaves
1 cup fresh basil leaves
Pinch salt
4 tablespoons olive oil

For the soup:

3 tablespoons unsalted butter
3 stalks celery, coarsely chopped*
6 apples (your favorite), peeled and diced*
2 pounds coarsely chopped celery root
1 bay leaf
1 yellow onion, coarsely chopped
1/2 cup all-purpose flour
3 quarts Homemade Chicken Stock (recipe, p. 234) or store-bought low-sodium
3 cups pure apple juice
2 cups heavy cream
5 russet potatoes, peeled and coarsely chopped
2 tablespoons granulated sugar
3 to 4 Roasted Fennel Bulbs (recipe, p. 201), coarsely chopped
Reserved juices from Roasted Fennel Bulbs
3 tablespoons cornstarch
Salt and pepper
Mint pesto

CHILLED COCONUT AND CURRIED CARROT SOUP

Serves 4

Sweet, spicy, savory — this satiny chilled soup boasts a complexity of flavors. I usually serve it chilled because the mild sweet nuttiness of the coconut milk makes it so refreshing. Garnished with basil cream, the soup not only looks beautiful but also tastes amazing.

What You Need

5-quart stockpot   Hand-held immersion blender   Standing blender
Large container   Plastic squeeze bottle   Medium-mesh strainer

How to Make

1. In the stockpot, lightly sauté* carrots, onion, ginger, sugar, curry paste, and bay leaf in oil over medium-high heat for about 4 to 5 minutes.
2. Add coconut milk and chicken stock. Bring to a boil; then turn down and simmer* over medium heat for 30 minutes.
3. Mix cornstarch with 1 tablespoon of water, blend well, and add to the soup. Simmer for 2 more minutes.
4. Pull off heat. Add lemon juice, salt, and pepper.
5. Purée well with a hand-held blender or in small batches with a standing blender. Pour through the strainer into the container. Let cool; then cover and refrigerate overnight.
6. The next day, prepare the basil cream. Place sour cream, basil leaves, lemon juice, and salt in the standing blender and blend well. Put basil cream into a squeeze bottle and set aside.
7. Check the thickness of the soup. If you prefer a lighter texture, thin the soup with a little water. For each serving, swirl a nice design on the soup with the basil cream and garnish with cilantro sprigs.

*See "chop," "sauté," "simmer," and "Thai curry paste" in the Glossary.

Ingredients

7 carrots, peeled and roughly chopped*
1/2 cup roughly chopped yellow onion
1 tablespoon chopped ginger
4 tablespoons granulated sugar
1 tablespoon Thai yellow curry paste*
1 bay leaf
2 tablespoons canola oil
1 13-1/2-ounce can natural coconut milk
1 quart plus 1 cup Homemade Chicken Stock (recipe, p. 234) or store-bought low-sodium
1 tablespoon cornstarch
1 tablespoon lemon juice
Salt and pepper to taste
1/2 cup sour cream
1/2 cup fresh basil leaves
1 teaspoon fresh lemon juice
Salt to taste
Cilantro sprigs

CLASSIC CREAM OF BROCCOLI SOUP

Serves 6 to 8

This classic soup is also a Toast favorite. So many of our customers love it that I thought I'd include it here. Simple and quick, when served with hot bread and a salad, it makes a meal in minutes.

What You Need

5-quart stockpot   Heavy-gauge whisk

How to Make

1. In the stockpot, melt butter and sauté* onions over medium-high heat until translucent, about 4 minutes.
2. Add flour and mix well with butter and onions, forming a roux.* The roux should be smooth and golden, not dry and lumpy. If it's too dry, add a little more butter or canola oil.
3. Add chicken stock, cream, milk, tarragon, bay leaf, and broccoli.
4. Bring to a boil, stirring from the bottom of the pot; then turn heat down to medium and continue to cook for about 25 to 30 minutes. Every couple of minutes, stir well from the bottom of the pot with the whisk and mash as you stir.
5. At this point, the mixture should be thick, with a semi-chunky consistency. Remove from heat. Add parsley, salt, pepper, Tabasco sauce, and lemon juice. Serve hot.

*See "chop," "dice," and "sauté" in the Glossary; for roux, see Tips and Techniques.

Ingredients

7 tablespoons unsalted butter
1 yellow onion, diced*
1-1/4 cups all-purpose flour
Canola oil
3 quarts Homemade Chicken Stock (recipe, p. 234) or store-bought low-sodium
1-1/2 cups heavy cream
1-1/2 cups milk
2 tablespoons chopped* fresh tarragon
1 bay leaf
6 cups chopped broccoli (both stems and florets)
1/4 cup chopped Italian parsley
Salt and pepper to taste
2 tablespoons Tabasco sauce
2 tablespoons lemon juice

FIVE-ONION SOUP

Serves 4 to 6

Based on the classic French onion soup, this five-onion version is simple to make. The trick is to be sure you caramelize the onions before deglazing the pot. That browning is the most important step in achieving the sumptuous flavors you want. Onion soup is one of my favorites, and this version teams perfectly with grilled cheese sandwiches.

What You Need

5-quart stockpot   Serving-size ovenproof bowls

How to Make

1. In the stockpot, melt butter over medium-low heat. Add Maui onions, leeks, yellow onions, shallots, red onions, and garlic and cook until well caramelized,* about 20 to 25 minutes.
2. Add tarragon, thyme, and basil and then deglaze* the pot with the sherry.
3. Add red wine and cook for 3 minutes over medium-high heat; then add beef stock and bay leaves and bring to a boil.
4. Turn down heat and cook soup at a medium-high simmer* for about 1 hour.
5. Add 1 tablespoon of water to the cornstarch, blend well, and add to the soup. Bring soup back to a boil over medium-high heat, cook for 1 minute more, and turn off heat. Texture should be chunky, and onions should be soft and smooth.
6. Remove bay leaves and add salt and pepper to taste.
7. To serve, put soup in ovenproof bowls, top with Crostini, and cover the bread completely with shredded Gruyère and Parmesan. Brown under the broiler. Serve immediately.

*See "caramelize," "chop," "deglaze," "dice," "Parmesan," and "simmer" in the Glossary.

Ingredients

3 tablespoons unsalted butter
2 Maui onions, coarsely chopped*
2 leeks, white and light green parts, diced*
2 medium yellow onions, coarsely chopped
1 cup coarsely chopped shallots
2 medium red onions, coarsely chopped
6 cloves garlic, peeled and sliced thin
2 tablespoons fresh tarragon
1 tablespoon fresh thyme
1 tablespoon dried basil
1 cup dry sherry
1 cup red wine (of a quality you'd like to drink)
3-1/2 quarts rich beef stock, homemade or store-bought
2 bay leaves
1 tablespoon cornstarch
Salt and pepper
1/4 cup chopped Italian parsley
Grated Gruyère and Parmesan,* enough to cover the soup in the serving bowls when melted
4 to 6 pieces Crostini (see Crostini and Croutons, p. 224), cut to fit the top of the bowls

CAULIFLOWER AND SWEET CORN SOUP

Serves 8 to 10

Try this hearty soup. It's as richly satisfying as a chowder, but lighter. Cauliflower and corn play well together, and the Roasted Tomato Compote lends the soup a more complex flavor.

What You Need

8-quart stockpot   Whisk

How to Make

1. In the pot, melt butter and sauté* onion, leeks, cumin, basil, celery, garlic, and corn.
2. Add flour and mix in well.
3. Add white wine, chicken stock, cream, potatoes, cauliflower, and bay leaf.
4. Bring to a boil; then turn down heat and simmer* for about 45 minutes, stirring from the bottom every few minutes.
5. When done, remove bay leaf and smash a little of the soup with the whisk to incorporate everything better.
6. Season with salt and pepper to taste and a dash of Tabasco sauce.
7. Garnish each bowl with a sprinkle of smoked paprika and some Roasted Tomato Compote and serve.

*See "chop," "dice," "sauté," and "simmer" in the Glossary.

Ingredients

1/3 pound unsalted butter
1 yellow onion, finely diced*
2 leeks, white and light green parts, washed thoroughly and finely diced
1/2 teaspoon ground cumin
1 tablespoon dried basil
2 stalks celery, finely diced
1 tablespoon chopped* garlic
3 cups sweet white corn kernels
1-1/2 cups all-purpose flour
1/2 cup white wine (of a quality you'd like to drink)
3 quarts Homemade Chicken Stock (recipe, p. 234) or store-bought low-sodium
2 cups heavy cream
5 russet potatoes, peeled and diced
4 cups chopped cauliflower
1 bay leaf
Salt and pepper
Tabasco sauce
1/2 teaspoon smoked paprika
Roasted Tomato Compote (recipe, p. 237)

HEIRLOOM TOMATO BREAD SOUP

Serves 4 to 6

This soup uses the ripest heirloom tomatoes, so it's best made in late summer or early autumn, when these luscious tomatoes are at their peak. The light soup is thickened with hearty chunks of tomato and bread and rounded out with fresh basil, olive oil, and nutty Grana Padano or Parmesan.

What You Need

4-quart stockpot   Cheese grater

How to Make

1. In the stockpot, add olive oil and sauté* onions, garlic, and tomatoes over medium heat until onions are translucent, about 4 minutes.
2. Add chicken stock, bread, basil, oregano, and bay leaf.
3. Bring to a boil; then turn down heat and simmer* for 30 minutes.
4. Add salt and pepper to taste and remove bay leaf.
5. Ladle into individual bowls and drizzle with olive oil. Shred Grana Padano on top and garnish with chopped parsley.

*See "chop," "dice," "Grana Padano," "Parmesan," "sauté," and "simmer" in the Glossary.

Ingredients

1/4 cup olive oil plus more for drizzling

1 medium yellow onion, finely diced*

6 garlic cloves, peeled and sliced thin

6 cups diced large ripe heirloom tomatoes

2 quarts Homemade Chicken Stock (recipe, p. 234) or store-bought low-sodium

2 cups diced day-old ciabatta, crusts trimmed off

1/2 cup chopped* fresh basil leaves

1 teaspoon fresh oregano

1 bay leaf

Salt and pepper

Grana Padano* or Parmesan*

Chopped parsley

LEEK AND POTATO SOUP

Serves 4 to 6

This is definitely a comfort soup — it always pleases with its soothing texture and warming flavors — and you'll find it unusually easy to make. Serve it with a green salad and hot bread for a simple dinner.

What You Need

5-quart stockpot

How to Make

1. In the stockpot, melt butter over medium-high heat and sauté* the leeks, onions, celery, garlic, tarragon, and basil until the vegetables sweat,* about 4 minutes.
2. Add flour and incorporate well; then cook for about 2 minutes or until the mixture is like a paste, making sure to scrape the corners of the pot.
3. Add wine, cream, and chicken stock and stir well to blend.
4. Add potatoes and bay leaf. Continue cooking at a high simmer,* stirring from the bottom periodically, for 30 minutes. Texture should be like a thick chowder.
5. When potatoes are soft enough to melt into the mixture, the soup is done. Remove from heat. Remove bay leaf and add a little Tabasco sauce, salt, and pepper. Garnish with green onions and chopped bacon (if using).

*See "chop," "dice," "sauté," "simmer," and "sweat" in the Glossary.

Ingredients

1/4 pound (1 stick) unsalted butter
3 leeks, white and some green parts, rinsed and diced*
1 large yellow onion, chopped*
2 stalks celery, finely diced
2 tablespoons chopped garlic
1 teaspoon tarragon
1 teaspoon basil
1 cup all-purpose flour
1/4 cup white wine (of a quality you'd like to drink)
2 cups heavy cream
3 quarts Homemade Chicken Stock (recipe, p. 234) or store-bought low-sodium
8 russet potatoes, peeled and diced
1 bay leaf
Tabasco sauce
Salt and pepper to taste
2 green onions, white and green parts, finely chopped
3 strips bacon, cooked and chopped (optional)

PORK AND PINTO BEAN SOUP

Serves 10 to 12

All-in-one-bowl meals tend to be hearty and comforting on a cold day. This one will really warm you up. Serve with a side of Cornbread with Jalapeño and Cheddar (recipe, p. 183). Optional garnishes of Salsa Fresca, avocado, cilantro, and Cotija cheese add flavors, textures, and color to this soup.

What You Need

Bowl for soaking beans   5-quart stockpot

How to Make

1. Soak beans in 6 cups of water for 2 to 3 hours.
2. Season pork with cumin, chili powder, and clove.
3. In the stockpot, heat olive oil over medium-high heat. Add pork and brown well, about 5 minutes on each side.
4. Drain oil and add onion, oregano, jalapeño chile, and garlic. Cook for 5 minutes.
5. Add chicken stock, bay leaf, and bones. Bring to a boil; then turn down heat to medium-low and simmer* for 45 minutes.
6. Add beans with their soaking water, cover, and continue to cook over medium-low heat for 1-1/2 hours. Continue adding water 1/2 quart at a time every few minutes until you have added 2-1/2 quarts. When beans are soft, the soup is done.
7. Remove bay leaf and then season with salt, pepper, and a little hot sauce to taste. (Optional: Garnish each serving with Salsa Fresca, diced avocado, cilantro, and Cotija cheese.)

*See "chop," "dice," "simmer," and "smash" in the Glossary.

Ingredients

4 cups dried pinto beans
6 cups water
3 pounds pork butt, with bone if possible, cut into 1-1/2-inch pieces (save bones for the soup)
1 teaspoon ground cumin
2 tablespoons chili powder
1 whole clove, ground
4 tablespoons olive oil
1 yellow onion, diced*
1 tablespoon oregano
1/2 jalapeño chile, seeded
4 cloves garlic, peeled and smashed*
4 quarts Homemade Chicken Stock (recipe, p. 234) or store-bought low-sodium
1 bay leaf
2-1/2 quarts water
Salt and pepper to taste
Hot sauce

Optional:

1/2 cup Salsa Fresca (recipe, p. 239)
2 avocados, diced
1/4 cup roughly chopped* cilantro
1/3 cup grated Cotija cheese

ROASTED GARLIC AND EGGPLANT SOUP

Serves 4 to 6

Silky, creamy, and slightly peppery, this aromatic vegetable soup also has hints of roasted garlic, cumin, oregano, and lemon. Its fundamentally light character makes it a pleasing year-round soup. I like to serve it with a drizzle of Basil Oil with chopped Roasted Tomatoes on top for garnish.

What You Need

5-quart stockpot   Hand-held immersion or standing blender   Large bowl
Cookie sheet

How to Make

Preheat oven to 375F.

1. In the large bowl, toss eggplant with olive oil, salt, and pepper. Lay the seasoned eggplant flat on a cookie sheet and bake for 20 to 25 minutes. Eggplant should look browned and be soft in the middle. Set aside.
2. In the stockpot, melt butter and caramelize* onions over medium heat for about 15 or 20 minutes.
3. Add sherry, chicken stock, roasted eggplant, cream, garbanzo beans, bay leaf, roasted garlic with roasting oil, curry powder, cumin, and oregano.
4. Bring to a boil over medium-high heat; then lower to medium and simmer* for about 30 minutes.
5. Mix cornstarch with 3 tablespoons of water, blend well, and add to the soup.
6. Simmer for a few more minutes; then remove from heat. Remove bay leaf and purée soup with a hand-held blender or in small batches in a standing blender.
7. Finish with lemon juice, Tabasco sauce, and salt and pepper to taste. (Optional: Top with a drizzle of Basil Oil or a dab of Pesto and 1 tablespoon of Roasted Tomatoes per bowl.) Serve immediately.

*See "caramelize," "chop," "dice," and "simmer" in the Glossary; for roasting garlic, see Tips and Techniques.

Ingredients

2 large eggplants with skin on, diced*
1/4 cup olive oil
Salt and pepper to taste
2 tablespoons butter
2 medium yellow onions, chopped*
1/4 cup dry sherry
2-1/2 quarts Homemade Chicken Stock (recipe, p. 234) or store-bought low-sodium
1/2 cup heavy cream
1 cup cooked garbanzo beans, strained (canned is OK)
1 bay leaf
1/2 cup roasted garlic* plus some of the roasting oil
1/2 teaspoon curry powder
1 teaspoon ground cumin
1 teaspoon dried oregano
3 tablespoons cornstarch
3 tablespoons lemon juice
1 tablespoon Tabasco sauce

Optional:
Basil Oil (recipe, p. 221) or Pesto (recipe, p. 235)
4 to 6 tablespoons peeled, chopped Roasted Tomatoes (recipe, p. 204)

SWEET PEA SOUP WITH HAM

Serves 4 to 6

Here's another soup that can be prepared quickly but still bursts with flavor and heartiness. It's a classic. Although most people use split peas, I prefer fresh or frozen peas because they give the soup a slightly sweeter flavor. Pair with plush, salty meats like ham, bacon, or prosciutto and garnish with Croutons (see Crostini and Croutons, p. 224) for an amazing result.

What You Need

4-quart stockpot   Hand-held immersion or standing blender

How to Make

1. In the stockpot, melt butter and sauté* onion, celery, carrots, bay leaf, tarragon, and basil until vegetables are soft.
2. Add flour and mix in well. If mixture looks too dry, add a little olive oil.
3. Add chicken stock and cream and bring to a boil over medium-high heat, stirring from the bottom of the pot.
4. Reduce heat, add peas, and simmer* over medium heat for 5 minutes.
5. Purée well with a hand-held blender or in small batches in a standing blender. If using a standard blender, return soup to the stockpot. Add lemon juice and ham.
6. Simmer for 5 more minutes and then serve.

*See "dice," "sauté," and "simmer" in the Glossary.

Ingredients

5 tablespoons unsalted butter
1 cup diced* yellow onion
2 celery stalks, diced
1 cup diced peeled carrots
1 bay leaf
1 tablespoon tarragon
1 tablespoon basil
1-1/3 cups all-purpose flour
Olive oil
2 quarts Homemade Chicken Stock (recipe, p. 234) or store-bought low-sodium
1/2 cup heavy cream
4 cups fresh or frozen peas
1 tablespoon lemon juice
1 cup diced ham

ASPARAGUS AND WATERCRESS SOUP

Serves 6 to 8

The flavors of fresh asparagus, peppery watercress, and tarragon are what this soup is all about. Its vegetal freshness, vibrant color, and crisp flavor are rewarding. Best of all, you can make this in just 15 minutes. Try it for a quick lunch or dinner with hot bread and sliced meats and cheeses.

What You Need

2 5-quart stockpots   Hand-held immersion or standing blender   Ice water

How to Make

1. Cut asparagus into 1-inch pieces, reserving 1 cup of the tips for garnish.
2. In a stockpot, blanch* the asparagus pieces in hot water for 30 seconds; then shock in ice water. Set aside.
3. In a stockpot, melt butter over medium heat and sauté* onions until they are translucent, about 2 to 3 minutes.
4. Add all the asparagus except the 1 cup of tips and sauté for 2 more minutes.
5. Add the flour and stir in well, making sure vegetables are coated. If the mixture looks too dry, add a little olive oil.
6. In the second stockpot over medium-high heat, bring the chicken stock, cream, and bay leaf to a boil.
7. Add the hot stock to the asparagus mixture and bring to a boil, making sure to stir from the bottom. It should thicken a little. Pull off the heat and remove bay leaf.
8. Add mint, tarragon, parsley, and watercress.
9. Purée until smooth with a hand-held blender or in small batches in a standing blender. Add lemon juice and season with salt and pepper to taste.
10. Garnish with asparagus tips and a little chopped parsley.

*See "chop," "dice," and "sauté" in the Glossary; for blanching, see Tips and Techniques.

Ingredients

2 pounds fresh asparagus, woody bottoms removed
5 tablespoons unsalted butter
1-1/2 cups diced* yellow onions
1-1/3 cups all-purpose flour
3 tablespoons olive oil (if needed)
2 quarts Homemade Chicken Stock (recipe, p. 234) or store-bought low-sodium
1 cup heavy cream
1 bay leaf
4 fresh mint leaves
1 bunch fresh tarragon, coarsely chopped*
1/4 cup chopped Italian parsley plus more for garnish
1 bunch whole watercress
3 tablespoons lemon juice
Salt and pepper

VEGETABLE AND WHITE BEAN SOUP

Serves 4

Thick, hearty, and comforting, this is a minestrone-style soup without the pasta (but you can always add some if you like). It's a nice way to get your kids to eat their vegetables. Topped with a little Grana Padano and served with hot sourdough bread, it's all you need for dinner.

What You Need

5-quart stockpot   Blender

How to Make

1. In the stockpot, add olive oil and sauté* carrots, celery, onions, zucchini, green beans, tomatoes, broccoli, cabbage, chard, garlic, basil, and oregano over medium-high heat until the vegetables soften, about 15 minutes.
2. Add tomato paste and cook for about 5 minutes.
3. Add the chicken stock, beans with their liquid, and bay leaf. Bring to a boil; then turn heat down to a high simmer* and cook for about 30 minutes.
4. Add potatoes and cook for another 15 minutes.
5. Mix cornstarch with 1 tablespoon of water, blend well, and add to the pot, stirring well.
6. Cook for 1 more minute; then pull off the heat.
7. Take out 3 to 4 cups of the soup and purée in the blender and then return puréed soup to the pot.
8. Add salt and pepper to taste. Top with a little grated Grana Padano and a drizzle of olive oil.

*See "chop," "dice," "Grana Padano," "sauté," and "simmer" in the Glossary.

Ingredients

4 tablespoons olive oil plus more for drizzling
4 carrots, peeled and diced*
3 stalks celery, diced
1 yellow onion, diced
3 green zucchini, diced
2 yellow zucchini, diced
1 cup green beans, cut in 1-inch pieces
2 cups chopped* tomatoes
2 cups chopped broccoli
2 cups chopped green cabbage
1 bunch Swiss chard, chopped
2 tablespoons chopped garlic
1/4 cup chopped fresh basil
1 tablespoon oregano
3 tablespoons tomato paste
3 quarts Homemade Chicken Stock (recipe, p. 234) or store-bought low-sodium
1 quart cooked cannellini beans with liquid (canned is OK)
1 bay leaf
3 russet potatoes, peeled and diced
1 tablespoon cornstarch
Salt and pepper
Grana Padano*

ROASTED CORN CHOWDER

Serves 4 to 6

This Southwestern-style corn chowder gets a little kick from chipotle chiles, and its smokiness is enhanced with a hint of lime and chili. I usually serve it with chopped poached prawns, Salsa Fresca (recipe, p. 239), diced avocado, and cilantro sprigs for a festive flair.

What You Need

Sheet pan   5-quart stockpot   Food processor or hand-held immersion blender

How to Make

Preheat oven to 400F.

1. On the sheet pan, lay out the corn, red and green bell peppers, and onion in a thin layer. Drizzle with olive oil.
2. Add cumin, chili powder, garlic, salt, and pepper and roast the vegetables until the edges are nicely browned, about 25 minutes. Set aside.
3. In the stockpot, bring chicken stock to a boil over medium-high heat. Add cream, bay leaf, and a pinch of oregano.
4. Add the roasted vegetables. Bring soup back to a boil and then reduce heat to medium and simmer* for 30 minutes.
5. Mix cornstarch with 2 tablespoons of cold water and add to the soup. Cook for a minute more; then turn off heat. Remove bay leaf.
6. Add cilantro, Cholula hot sauce, and lime juice and purée well in the food processor.
7. Season with salt and pepper and serve immediately.

*See "Cholula hot sauce," "chop," "dice," "simmer," and "smash" in the Glossary.

Ingredients

6 cups fresh sweet white corn (frozen is OK)
1 red bell pepper, seeded, peeled, and roughly chopped*
1 green bell pepper, seeded, peeled, and roughly chopped
1/2 red onion, diced*
4 tablespoons olive oil
1 teaspoon ground cumin
2 tablespoons chili powder
4 cloves garlic, peeled and smashed*
Salt and pepper to taste
3 quarts Homemade Chicken Stock (recipe, p. 234) or store-bought low-sodium
1 cup heavy cream
1 bay leaf
Oregano
2 tablespoons cornstarch
1 to 2 chipotle chiles (depending on how hot you like it)
1/3 cup chopped cilantro
3 tablespoons Cholula hot sauce*
Juice of 2 limes

TURKEY CHILI

Serves 4

This turkey-based chili is as healthful as it is good, and people order it year-round at our restaurants. I like to serve it with cheddar cheese, chopped tomatoes, onions, sour cream, and cilantro. Or try it topped with eggs or in omelets. There are many ways to enjoy this versatile dish.

What You Need

4-quart stockpot   Grater

How to Make

Preheat oven to 375F.

1. In the stockpot, heat oil over medium-high heat. Add turkey and brown for about 10 to 15 minutes; then add the chili powder, a pinch of cayenne, onions, bell pepper, and chipotle and Serrano chiles.
2. Cook until everything is well incorporated, about 5 minutes.
3. Add the crushed tomatoes, diced tomatoes, and tomato paste. Cook until mixture is slightly caramelized,* about 15 minutes.
4. Add the chicken stock, beans with their liquid, oregano, bay leaf, curry powder, and cumin and cook over medium-high heat for about 5 minutes; then turn down to medium heat and simmer* until thick, 45 minutes to 1 hour, stirring often from the bottom.
5. Remove bay leaf. Add Cholula hot sauce, salt, and pepper and serve. (Optional: Garnish with cheddar cheese, tomatoes, sour cream, red onions, and cilantro.)

*See "caramelize," "chop," "Cholula hot sauce," "dice," and "simmer" in the Glossary.

Ingredients

3 tablespoons olive oil
1-1/2 pounds ground turkey
1 tablespoon chili powder
Cayenne pepper
1/2 cup diced* yellow onion
1/2 cup diced green bell pepper
1 to 2 chipotle chiles, chopped*
1 roasted serrano chile, peeled, seeded, and chopped
1 cup canned crushed tomatoes
3 cups diced tomatoes
1/3 cup tomato paste
2 cups Homemade Chicken Stock (recipe, p. 234) or store-bought low-sodium
6 cups Pinto Beans (recipe, p. 189) with their liquid
1 teaspoon oregano
1 bay leaf
1 teaspoon curry powder
1/2 teaspoon ground cumin
2 tablespoons Cholula hot sauce* or your favorite hot sauce
Salt and pepper to taste

Optional:
1-1/2 cups shredded cheddar cheese
1 cup chopped tomatoes
1/2 cup sour cream
1/3 cup diced red onions
1/3 cup roughly chopped cilantro

LAMB STEW WITH BRAISED FENNEL, MASHED POTATOES, AND CARAMELIZED CARROTS

Serves 4

Here's a little twist on the traditional lamb stew — it's cooked with fennel, which I find unusually complementary to lamb, and balanced with the mellow sweetness of caramelized carrots. Serve with Roasted Fennel Bulbs (recipe, p. 201) and Mashed Potatoes (recipe, p. 191).

What You Need

Cookie sheet   5-quart stockpot   9 x 13-inch roasting pan   12-inch frying pan

How to Make

FOR THE CARAMELIZED CARROTS:

Preheat oven to 375F.

1. Toss carrots with olive oil and salt and pepper to taste.
2. Lay out on the cookie sheet, leaving a little space around each piece of carrot.
3. Roast, stirring every so often till carrots are soft and have a caramelized color, about 15 minutes.

FOR THE LAMB STEW:

Preheat oven to 375F.

1. Season the lamb with salt and pepper.
2. In the frying pan over medium heat, add the butter. As soon as it melts, lower heat to low and slow-cook the onions until they caramelize,* about 12 to 15 minutes.
3. In the roasting pan, add olive oil over medium-high heat; then add lamb chunks, making sure not to crowd the meat. Brown well, about 15 minutes.
4. Add flour and mix until lamb chunks are well coated.
5. Add fennel and caramelized onions with their juices to the pan.
6. Add tomatoes, lamb stock, wine, garlic, bay leaf, and celery stalks. Cover and put in the oven. Cook until the sauce has thickened slightly and the meat is pillow-tender, about 2-1/2 hours.
7. Remove bay leaf and celery stalks.
8. Divide stew and caramelized carrots among four plates. Garnish with fennel sprigs.

*See "caramelize," "chop," and "dice" in the Glossary.

Ingredients

For the caramelized carrots:

4 carrots, peeled and cut into
    3 x 1/2-inch sticks
3 tablespoons olive oil
Salt and black pepper

For the lamb stew:

3 pounds leg of lamb, cut into
    chunks about 1 inch in size
Salt and pepper
3 tablespoons unsalted butter
2 yellow onions, diced*
1/4 cup olive oil
1 cup all-purpose flour
1 fennel bulb, chopped* fine
    (save sprigs for garnish)
2 cups canned crushed toma-
    toes or peeled, crushed fresh
    tomatoes
3 cups lamb stock (see veal
    stock in Basic Demi-glace,
    p. 228, and use lamb bones
    instead)
2 cups white wine (of a quality
    you'd like to drink)
2 tablespoons chopped garlic
1 bay leaf
2 celery stalks, cut in half

SALADS

SALADS

Salads have really evolved over the past twenty years, moving way beyond the 1950s- and 1960s-style standard of iceberg lettuce and blue cheese dressing. In the twenty-first century, salads are artful compositions of fresh fruits, vegetables, and meats bound together with imaginative dressings. They're served as appetizers and palate cleansers as well as lunch and dinner entrées, especially in season.

In California, there are at least seven months of the year when the bounty of fresh vegetables and fruits not only plays well on the palate but pleases the whole body and mind. Use these recipes as blueprints to guide you in making dressings and marrying flavors. Then try your own ideas. Be creative, and let the fresh flavors of the ingredients speak for themselves.

TOAST CAESAR

Serves 4

Caesar salad is a classic dish. The zesty combination of garlic, anchovy, Grana Padano (or a good Parmesan) brought together with the zing of lemon and the richness of olive oil is irresistible. Add some grilled chicken, prawns, steak, or even meatballs to make it a full meal.

   This is our version. The dressing can be made a day ahead and refrigerated.

What You Need

Food processor   Large bowl

How to Make

FOR THE DRESSING:

1. In the food processor, add coddled egg yolks, mustard, Worcestershire sauce, vinegar, lemon juice, Tabasco sauce, salt, anchovies, and garlic.
2. With the processor running, slowly drizzle in the olive and canola oils. The dressing should become thick and emulsified.
3. Add Grana Padano and pepper and check for seasoning. The dressing should taste salty and tangy. Add more garlic or anchovy if you prefer.

FOR THE SALAD:

1. Chill four large plates. In the bowl, gently toss the lettuce with the dressing, lemon juice, Croutons, salt, and pepper. Make sure each piece of lettuce is coated with dressing.
2. Divide equally among chilled plates and garnish with Grana Padano and more anchovy fillets if you wish.

*See "Grana Padano," "Parmesan," and "smash" in the Glossary; for coddling, see Tips and Techniques.

Ingredients

For the dressing (makes about 2-1/2 cups):

4 egg yolks, coddled*
1 tablespoon Dijon mustard
3 tablespoons Worcestershire sauce
1/4 cup red wine vinegar
1/4 cup lemon juice
1 tablespoon Tabasco sauce
1 teaspoon kosher salt
4 anchovy fillets (packed in olive oil, not salt)
4 garlic cloves, peeled and smashed*
1/3 cup and 2 tablespoons olive oil
2/3 cup and 2 tablespoons canola oil
3/4 cup grated Grana Padano* or Parmesan*
1/2 teaspoon freshly ground black pepper

For the salad:

4 romaine lettuce hearts, washed, dried, and cut into 1-1/2-inch squares (or whole leaves if you prefer)
3/4 cup dressing
Juice of 1/2 lemon
2 cups Croutons (see Crostini and Croutons, p. 224)
Salt and pepper to taste
1/2 cup shaved Grana Padano or Parmesan
Anchovy fillets (optional)

WARM SPINACH SALAD WITH BACON VINAIGRETTE

Serves 4

Savory and full-bodied, this salad combines lightly wilted spinach and radicchio with bacon, pickled red onions, Asiago, and water chestnuts for a little extra texture. You can make it even more substantial by adding grilled chicken or steak. On its own, it's a fine first course or light meal.

What You Need

12-inch frying pan   Large bowl

How to Make

1. Pickle sliced onion in rice vinegar, sugar, and a pinch of salt. Set aside.
2. Wash and dry radicchio and spinach.
3. In the frying pan, add 1 tablespoon of olive oil and bacon. Cook bacon over medium heat until it begins to get brown but not crispy, about 10 minutes.
4. Remove about two-thirds of the bacon fat and add shallots and garlic.
5. Cook for about 10 seconds; then add radicchio.
6. Cook, stirring constantly, for about 10 seconds and add the balsamic vinegar at the last second.
7. Put mixture into the large bowl and quickly add spinach, salt, pepper, 3 tablespoons olive oil, half the Asiago, and water chestnuts and toss, mixing everything well. The hot bacon and oil should wilt the spinach.
8. Place equal amounts on four plates. Top each serving with more Asiago, pine nuts, pickled red onions, and 2 Roasted Tomato halves. Serve immediately.

*See "chop" in the Glossary; for toasting, see Tips and Techniques.

Ingredients

1/2 red onion, thinly sliced

3 tablespoons seasoned rice vinegar

1/2 teaspoon granulated sugar

Salt

1 head radicchio, chopped*

1 pound baby spinach, washed and dried

4 tablespoons extra-virgin olive oil

4 strips thick bacon or pancetta, cooked and chopped

2 tablespoons chopped shallots

1/2 teaspoon chopped garlic

1/4 cup aged balsamic vinegar

Salt and pepper to taste

3/4 cup grated Asiago

3/4 cup canned, sliced water chestnuts, rinsed and dried

1/4 cup toasted* pine nuts

8 halves Roasted Tomatoes (recipe, p. 204)

CHICKEN APPLE SALAD

Serves 4

Apples marry well with the shaved fennel and Champagne Vinaigrette that give this salad a nice zip. I like to use Fuji apples because they are crisp, sweet, and consistent in texture. Other varieties will work, too, but just stay away from apples that are too tart or mushy.

Shave the fennel very thin so its flavor doesn't overwhelm the salad. I use a Japanese mandoline, but a French mandoline, a slicer, or a good sharp knife will also do the trick. A nice Gorgonzola is also important to this dish. You can substitute Maytag Blue Cheese or something similar, as long as the cheese is not too pungent.

This salad works well as a luncheon entrée. Without the chicken, it makes a nice starter for a spring or summer dinner. And for something a little different but equally harmonious, try this recipe with figs instead of apples.

What You Need

Mandoline   Large bowl

How to Make

1. Chill four large plates or salad bowls. In the large bowl, add salad greens, romaine lettuce, fennel, chicken, and apple. Add Champagne Vinaigrette, salt, and pepper and toss gently.
2. Lay 1 radicchio leaf on each plate. Portion out the salad equally onto the leaves. Top with Candied Walnuts, Gorgonzola, and 1 Crostini each. (If using figs instead of apples, toss the figs separately with a little vinaigrette, salt, and pepper; then place on and around the salad.) Serve immediately.

*See "chop" and "julienne" in the Glossary; for grilling, see Tips and Techniques.

Ingredients

12 ounces spring mix salad greens (around 4 large handfuls), washed and dried

1 romaine lettuce heart, cut into 1-inch pieces

1/2 fennel bulb, shaved with a mandoline

4 4-ounce chicken breasts, grilled* and julienned*

2 Fuji apples, sliced thinly into equal-size pieces (or 16 black or green figs, halved)

1/2 cup Champagne Vinaigrette (recipe, p. 231)

Salt and pepper to taste

1/2 cup chopped* Candied Walnuts (recipe, p. 222)

1/3 cup crumbled Gorgonzola

4 large radicchio leaves (ends cut off and soaked in water to clean leaves thoroughly)

4 Crostini (see Crostini and Croutons, p. 224)

CALAMARI SALAD WITH NAPA CABBAGE AND CANNELLINI BEANS

Serves 4

Napa cabbage is a wonderful green for cooking or using in salads. This recipe combines the mild, crisp cabbage with spicy calamari, creamy cannellini beans, red onions, cherry tomatoes, and basil. Serve it as an appetizer or a light dinner with a side of grilled bread.

What You Need

5-quart stockpot   Bowl for marinating calamari   Large bowl   Ice cubes

How to Make

FOR THE CALAMARI:

1. Fill the stockpot with water, add salt to taste, and bring to a boil. Add the calamari and cook for about 30 seconds; then remove and plunge into an ice bath (made with water and ice cubes). Shake off excess water and drain well.
2. Toss calamari in the bowl with the Thai curry paste, olive oil, lemon juice, garlic, lemongrass, and a pinch each of salt and pepper. Cover and refrigerate overnight.

FOR THE SALAD:

1. Remove lemongrass from the marinated calamari.
2. In the large bowl, toss the marinated calamari with the salad ingredients, balsamic vinegar, olive oil, and lemon juice. Season with salt and pepper to taste.
3. Serve family-style on a large platter or on individual plates.

*See "chop" and "Thai curry paste" in the Glossary.

Ingredients

For the calamari:

1-1/2 pounds calamari tubes and
    tentacles, cleaned and cut
    into 1/2-inch pieces
Salt and pepper
1 tablespoon Thai red curry
    paste*
3 tablespoons extra-virgin olive oil
Juice of 2 lemons
1 tablespoon chopped* garlic
1 stalk fresh lemongrass, split
    and cut into 3-inch pieces

For the salad:

1-1/2 pounds marinated calamari
1 head napa cabbage, chopped
    into 1/4-inch shreds
1/2 red onion, thinly sliced
1 cup halved cherry tomatoes
2 cups cooked cannellini beans,
    strained (canned is OK)
1/2 cup chopped Italian parsley
1/4 cup chives, cut into 1-inch
    pieces
1/2 cup whole fresh basil leaves,
    stems removed
1/4 cup white balsamic vinegar
1/4 cup extra-virgin olive oil
Juice of 1 lemon
Salt and pepper

AUTUMN CHICKEN SALAD

Serves 4

This salad sings of autumn with its resonant mix of chilled roasted butternut and acorn squashes, pears, pomegranate, green beans, grilled chicken, red grapes, candied pecans, and curried vinaigrette. The festive presentation makes it ideal for any October or November celebration. Or you could omit the chicken and serve as a starter salad for Thanksgiving dinner. Everything can be prepared the day before.

What You Need

Mixing bowl   Whisk   Roasting pan   Vegetable peeler
Deep-fryer or 12-inch deep-sided skillet   Large bowl

How to Make

FOR THE YELLOW CURRY VINAIGRETTE:

In the mixing bowl, whisk together all the ingredients and let sit for about 15 minutes before using. Dressing can be refrigerated for up to a week.

FOR THE SQUASHES:

Preheat oven to 350F.

1. Cut the squashes in half and clean out the seeds. Take one of the butternut squash halves and make 1-inch-wide ribbons with a vegetable peeler. Set aside.
2. Rub the cavities of the squash halves with olive oil, brown sugar, salt, and pepper. Place in the roasting pan.
3. Roast squashes until fork-tender but not mushy, about 1 hour. Remove from oven and let cool.
4. In the deep-fryer, heat canola oil to 300F. Oil should be about 1/2 inch deep. Add squash ribbons and fry* until crispy, about 3 minutes. Drain on a towel and season with salt.
5. When roasted squashes are cool, peel the butternut squash and cut into 1-inch cubes. Leave the skin on the acorn squash and cut into 2-inch wedges. Place both in the refrigerator to chill.

Ingredients

For the yellow curry vinaigrette (makes about 1-1/2 cups):

1/2 cup seasoned rice vinegar
1 tablespoon very finely chopped* ginger
1 cup plus 2 tablespoons mayonnaise
1 tablespoon Thai yellow curry paste*
1 teaspoon yellow curry powder
1 tablespoon chopped parsley
1 tablespoon honey

For the squashes:

1-1/2 to 2 pounds butternut squash, enough to yield 2 cups cooked
1 large acorn squash (2 if small)
1/4 cup olive oil
1 tablespoon brown sugar
Canola oil
Salt and pepper to taste

FOR THE SALAD:

1. Arrange two or three acorn squash wedges on each of four plates.
2. In the large bowl, toss salad greens, grapes, French green beans, chicken, red onion, butternut squash, and pears with the curry vinaigrette, making sure everything is well coated. Salt and pepper to taste.
3. Place equal amounts of the salad mixture on top of the acorn squash slices. Top with pomegranate seeds, pecans, fried sage leaves, and butternut squash ribbons. Serve immediately.

*See "chop," "julienne," and "Thai curry paste" in the Glossary; for blanching, frying, and grilling, see Tips and Techniques.

Ingredients continued

For the salad:

Roasted acorn squash wedges

1 pound spring mix salad greens

1 cup halved red seedless grapes

6 ounces French green beans, stemmed and blanched*

1 pound grilled* chicken, julienned* into 1/4-inch-wide strips

1/2 red onion, thinly sliced

2 cups roasted butternut squash cubes

2 crisp Bosc pears or red pears, stems and seeds removed, thinly sliced

1 to 1-1/2 cups curry vinaigrette

Salt and pepper

1 cup fresh pomegranate seeds

1/2 cup chopped candied pecans (see Candied Walnuts, p. 222)

1 bunch fried sage leaves (see Fried Fresh Herbs, p. 225)

Fried butternut squash ribbons

CHINESE ALMOND CHICKEN SALAD

Serves 4

This may be one of Marin's most popular salads. Just about everybody, from professional chef to home cook, has his or her own version. Ours is very light, enriched with toasted almonds, crispy rice noodles, mandarin oranges, and ginger vinaigrette. This salad is a Toast favorite precisely because it is so light and flavorful.

Prepare the chicken the day before, so all you'll have to do is assemble the salad when you want to serve it. If you use a gas grill or barbecue instead of a grill pan, the chicken will be even more flavorful. Fresh satsuma mandarin oranges are a nice touch, but if you can't find them, canned will do.

What You Need

Deep-fryer or 12-inch deep-sided skillet and cooking thermometer
Blender   Grill pan   Strainer   Large plate   Large bowl

How to Make

FOR THE GINGER VINAIGRETTE:

1. In the blender, add vinegar, ginger, garlic, sugar, and honey.
2. With the blender running, drizzle in the sesame and canola oils.
3. Add salt and pepper to taste and refrigerate until needed.

FOR THE CHICKEN AND CRISPY RICE NOODLES:

1. In the bowl, mix ginger, green onion, garlic, sambal, brown sugar, sesame and canola oils, soy sauce, and chicken breasts together well, making sure chicken is fully soaked. Cover and refrigerate overnight.
2. Spray a layer of PAM cooking spray on the grill pan. Heat to medium-high.
3. Evenly lay out the chicken breasts. Cook for 3 minutes; then rotate and continue to cook the same side for another 3 minutes. Flip each piece of chicken and continue to cook for another 4 to 5 minutes. The whole process should take about 10 minutes.
4. Remove from heat, let cool for 15 minutes, and then julienne. Make sure chicken is no longer warm before assembling the salad.
5. Line the large plate with paper towels.
6. Heat the deep-fryer or oil to exactly 400F and then add rice noodles. They will puff up quickly when they hit the hot oil. As soon as they've stopped puffing up, remove with the strainer and place in the paper-towel-lined plate to drain.

Ingredients

For the ginger vinaigrette
(makes about 2 cups):

3/4 cup seasoned rice vinegar
1/4 cup finely chopped ginger*
3 garlic cloves, peeled and
   crushed
2 tablespoons granulated sugar
1 tablespoon honey
1/4 cup sesame oil
1 cup canola oil
Salt and pepper

FOR THE SALAD:

1. Divide crispy rice noodles among four serving bowls.
2. In the large bowl, toss the lettuce, carrots, chicken, bean sprouts, 1/2 cup of almonds, green onion, and vinaigrette. Salt and pepper to taste.
3. Divide salad evenly among the bowls.
4. Top with sesame seeds, cilantro sprigs, 1/2 cup almonds, and mandarin oranges.

*See "chop," "julienne," "PAM cooking spray," and "sambal" in the Glossary; for cutting on the bias, grilling, and toasting, see Tips and Techniques.

Ingredients continued

For the chicken and crispy rice noodles:

1 tablespoon coarsely chopped ginger
1 tablespoon finely chopped green onion, white and green parts
1 teaspoon finely chopped garlic
1/2 teaspoon sambal*
1 tablespoon brown sugar
1 tablespoon sesame oil
1 tablespoon canola oil
2 tablespoons light soy sauce
4 6-ounce skinless and boneless chicken breasts
PAM cooking spray*
1 cup dried rice noodles (saifun), well separated
2 cups Crisco or vegetable oil

For the salad:

Crispy rice noodles
4 romaine lettuce hearts, chopped into strips
1/2 cup finely julienned* carrots
4 julienned grilled* chicken breasts
2 cups bean sprouts
1 cup toasted* sliced almonds
1/2 cup green onion, white and green parts, cut thin on the bias*
3/4 cup ginger vinaigrette
Salt and pepper
2 tablespoons toasted sesame seeds
Cilantro sprigs
1 cup mandarin orange segments

CHICKEN WATERMELON SALAD

Serves 4 to 6

This unusual and refreshing salad has become one of the most popular dishes at Toast. With its sweet, rosy watermelon, daikon, grilled chicken, bean sprouts, and wonton strips, it offers a distinctive and exciting assortment of flavors and textures. The peanut vinaigrette is an Asian-inspired dressing that really brings this dish together.

The salad is best served in the summer, when watermelons are at their peak. If you'd rather not deep-fry wonton strips, store-bought crispy Asian noodles will do. For the lettuce, I favor chopped romaine, but iceberg works well, too. Make sure the watermelon is ripe and the bean sprouts are fresh, with a good snap. Daikon (a Japanese radish) is pretty easy to find, so do not substitute for this ingredient or you could end up with a completely different dish. Preparing the chicken the day before will make assembling the salad faster and easier. Cooking the chicken on a gas grill will add an extra dimension of flavor.

What You Need

Deep-fryer with strainer or 12-inch deep-sided skillet and cooking thermometer
Food processor   Tongs   Large plate   2 large bowls   Mandoline
Grill pan or cast iron frying pan

How to Make

FOR THE PEANUT VINAIGRETTE:

1. In the food processor, add vinegar, honey, ginger, cilantro, green onion, and peanut butter. Blend well.
2. With the processor running, slowly drizzle in the sesame and canola oils; then add a little salt to taste. Set aside.

Ingredients

For the peanut vinaigrette
   (makes 2 cups):

1 cup seasoned rice vinegar
1/4 cup honey
1-1/2 tablespoons finely diced*
   peeled ginger
2 tablespoons chopped* cilantro
2 green onions, white and green
   parts, roughly chopped
3/4 cup creamy peanut butter
3 tablespoons sesame oil
1 cup canola oil
Salt

FOR THE CHICKEN AND WONTON STRIPS:

1. In a large bowl, mix marinade ingredients and chicken breasts together, making sure chicken is fully soaked. Cover and refrigerate overnight.
2. Spray a layer of PAM cooking spray on the grill pan. Heat to medium-high.
3. Evenly lay out the chicken breasts. Cook for 3 minutes; then rotate and continue to cook the same side for another 3 minutes. Flip each piece of chicken and continue to cook for another 4 to 5 minutes. The whole grilling process should take about 10 minutes.
4. Remove from heat, let cool for 15 minutes, and then julienne. Make sure chicken is no longer warm before assembling the salad.
5. Line the plate with paper towels and set aside.
6. Heat the deep-fryer or oil to 350F.
7. Separate wonton wrappers and cut each into 1/4-inch strips. Dust with a little flour so they don't stick together.
8. Fry* strips in small batches, moving around with the tongs, until they're golden brown. Remove with tongs to the paper-towel-lined plate to drain.

FOR THE SALAD:

1. Chill four large salad plates or bowls.
2. In a large bowl, combine lettuce, watermelon, daikon, 1 cup of wonton strips, carrots, half the peanuts, chicken, bean sprouts, and peanut vinaigrette. Toss gently.
3. Divide evenly among plates or bowls. Garnish with the rest of the peanuts, 1 cup wonton strips, black sesame seeds, and cilantro sprigs.

*See "chop," "dice," "julienne," "PAM cooking spray," and "sambal" in the Glossary; for frying, grilling, and toasting, see Tips and Techniques.

Ingredients continued

For the chicken and wonton strips:

4 6-ounce skinless and boneless chicken breasts
1 tablespoon coarsely chopped ginger
1 tablespoon finely chopped green onion, white and green parts
1 teaspoon finely chopped garlic
1/2 teaspoon sambal*
1 tablespoon brown sugar
1 tablespoon sesame oil
1 tablespoon canola oil
2 tablespoons light soy sauce
PAM cooking spray*
15 to 18 wonton wrappers
2 cups Crisco or vegetable oil
Flour

For the salad:

4 romaine lettuce hearts (including the small, crisp centers), chopped
2 cups julienned* watermelon
1 cup julienned daikon
2 cups wonton strips (less if using store-bought crispy Asian noodles)
1/2 cup finely julienned carrot
1/3 cup chopped honey-roasted peanuts
Grilled* chicken breasts, julienned
1 cup bean sprouts
1 cup peanut vinaigrette
2 tablespoons toasted* black sesame seeds
Cilantro sprigs

ARTICHOKE AND PRAWN PANZANELLA SALAD

Serves 4

Panzanella is an Italian bread salad. It's a delicious as well as thrifty concoction. Like bread pudding, it comes from the European tradition of finding creative ways of using up day-old bread. This version adds poached prawns and is presented in chilled, hollowed-out artichokes.

I truly love artichokes, and this dish puts them at center stage. The artichokes, prawns, and Croutons can all be prepared a day ahead. Serve with a side of Lemon-Basil Aioli (recipe, p. 241) for extra zest.

What You Need

8- to 10-quart stockpot with lid   2-quart saucepan   Sheet pan   Large bowl
Kitchen shears

How to Make

FOR THE ARTICHOKES:

1. Cut a little bit off the stem and then slice off the top quarter of the artichokes. With the kitchen shears, cut off the thorn on each leaf.
2. In the stockpot, set the artichokes tightly together, stem side up. Add enough water to just cover the artichokes. Add kosher salt, olive oil, and lemon half.
3. Cover the artichokes with a sheet of wax paper and weigh them down with a heat-resistant plate.
4. Cover the pot and cook the artichokes over medium-high heat until a fork easily pierces the bottom of each one, about 25 to 30 minutes.
5. Remove from the pot and set artichokes to cool on the sheet pan, stem side up. Chill four plates.
6. With a tablespoon, scoop out the middles of the cooled artichokes until they resemble bowls and cut off the stems.
7. Set one on each of the four plates.

Ingredients

For the artichokes:

4 large artichokes
2 to 3 tablespoons kosher salt
2 tablespoons olive oil
1/2 lemon

For the prawns:

16 prawns, with shells on
1-1/2 quarts water
1/2 lemon
1 tablespoon pickling spices

FOR THE PRAWNS:

1. In the saucepan, add 1-1/2 quarts of water, juice and peel of 1/2 lemon, and pickling spices.
2. Bring water to a boil over medium-high heat and reduce* for 10 minutes.
3. Poach* the prawns in their shells in the reduced liquid for 2-1/2 to 3 minutes. They should not be opaque. Remove and lay them out on the sheet pan to cool.
4. Remove shells, devein,* and slice lengthwise into 1/2-inch pieces.

FOR THE SALAD:

1. In the bowl, toss the Croutons, sliced prawns, tomatoes, onion, basil, artichoke hearts, pine nuts, romaine lettuce, olive oil, and red wine vinaigrette together. Season with salt and pepper to taste.
2. Fill artichokes with the salad, stuffing each one well.
3. Garnish with Grana Padano, parsley, and lemon wedges.

*See "chiffonade," "chop," "Grana Padano," and "reduce" in the Glossary; for deveining, poaching, and toasting, see Tips and Techniques.

Ingredients continued

For the salad:

1 cup freshly made Croutons
(see Crostini and Croutons,
p. 224)
2 vine-ripened tomatoes, cut in
1-inch chunks
1/4 cup chopped* red onion
1/4 cup chiffonade* of fresh basil
1/2 cup marinated artichoke
hearts, drained
1/4 cup toasted* pine nuts
1 romaine lettuce heart,
chopped into 1/2-inch pieces
2 tablespoons extra-virgin olive oil
1/2 cup red wine vinaigrette
(see Champagne Vinaigrette,
p. 231)
Salt and pepper
4 prepared artichokes
1/4 cup shaved Grana Padano*
1/4 cup chopped parsley
Lemon wedges

BARBECUED SPICED PRAWN SALAD

Serves 4

Want an ideal summertime barbecue dish? Try this salad topped with spicy, smoky prawns, best served at sunset next to a beautiful ocean view. Everything can be prepared ahead of time and then simply grilled and heated when you're ready. Cornbread with Jalapeño and Cheddar heightens the flavors of this warm, Cajun-influenced salad.

What You Need

4 12-inch bamboo skewers   Grill   12-inch frying pan

How to Make

FOR THE PRAWNS:

1. Soak bamboo skewers in water for 24 hours.
2. Mix together all the ingredients and thoroughly coat the prawns.
3. Skewer the prawns from head to tail, 6 on a skewer, and marinate at least 4 hours or overnight.
4. Heat grill to medium-high. Place the skewered prawns on the grill and season with salt and pepper. Grill* for 2-1/2 minutes on each side, squeezing a little lemon juice on the prawns while they're grilling. When they feel slightly firm but not tough, they're done.
5. Pull off grill and set aside.

Ingredients

For the prawns:

24 prawns shelled, deveined,* tails on
1/4 cup ketchup
1 tablespoon brown sugar
1/4 teaspoon cayenne pepper
1 tablespoon onion powder
1 tablespoon garlic powder
2 tablespoons Worcestershire sauce
1 tablespoon ancho chile powder
2 tablespoons Cholula hot sauce*
Salt and pepper to taste
Lemon juice

FOR THE SALAD:

1. Set the frying pan on the grill and let it get thoroughly hot.
2. Add olive oil and andouille sausage. Cook until the sausage begins to sputter; then add onion, garlic, chili powder, cumin, and corn and sauté* for 2 minutes.
3. Add potatoes and cook until mixture is warm.
4. Add tomatoes, mustard, beans, and vinegar and cook until combined, another 2 minutes.
5. Add salt, pepper, and spinach and toss quickly just until spinach is wilted.
6. Cut the pieces of Cornbread with Jalapeño and Cheddar in half and grill until each has a nice brown crust.
7. Place 2 halves of the grilled cornbread on each of four plates. Place equal amounts of the hot salad in the middle of each plate; then rest a skewer of prawns on top. Serve immediately and enjoy the sunset.

*See "chop," "dice," "Cholula hot sauce," and "sauté" in the Glossary; for blanching, deveining, and grilling, see Tips and Techniques.

Ingredients continued

For the salad:

4 tablespoons olive oil
1 cup diced* andouille sausage
1/4 cup diced red onion
1 tablespoon chopped* garlic
1/2 teaspoon chili powder
1/4 teaspoon ground cumin
2 cups uncooked sweet corn
   kernels
2 cups sliced cooked fingerling
   potatoes
2 cups ripe heirloom tomatoes,
   cut in chunks
2 tablespoons Creole mustard
6 ounces blanched* French
   green beans
1/4 cup sherry vinegar
Salt and pepper to taste
1/2 pound baby spinach
4 pieces Cornbread with
   Jalapeño and Cheddar
   (recipe, p. 183)
Juice of 1 lemon

PEPPER-CRUSTED AHI SALAD WITH TRUFFLE VINAIGRETTE

Serves 4

This salad is all about vibrant colors and earthy, fresh character. The truffle-infused vinaigrette complements the tuna with its subtle flavor. Preparation is simple enough that you can enjoy this salad any day of the week. Almost all of it can be made the day before, except for the tuna.

What You Need

Mixing bowl   Whisk   10-inch frying pan   Mandoline   Large bowl

How to Make

FOR THE TRUFFLE VINAIGRETTE:

In the bowl, whisk the vinegar, lemon juice, shallots, mustard, and honey together while slowly drizzling in the oils. Add salt and pepper to taste.

FOR THE SALAD:

1. In the frying pan, add oil over medium-high heat. Season ahi with salt and then encrust one side with peppercorns. Sear peppered side first, about 3 minutes; then sear the other side, about 3 minutes more. Set aside.
2. In the bowl, toss salad greens and frisée with asparagus, tomatoes, potatoes, onion, chives, parsley, 1/2 cup of truffle vinaigrette, salt, and pepper.
3. Divide salad equally among four plates. Slice each tuna steak and fan slices across the top of each salad. Drizzle a little more vinaigrette on the side and serve immediately.

*See "chop" in the Glossary; for blanching, see Tips and Techniques.

Ingredients

For the truffle vinaigrette (makes about 1 cup):

1/4 cup champagne vinegar
2 tablespoons lemon juice
2 tablespoons chopped* shallots
1 tablespoon whole-grain mustard
1 tablespoon honey
1/4 cup truffle oil
1/2 cup canola oil
Salt and pepper

For the salad:

3 tablespoons olive oil
4 5-ounce ahi tuna steaks, about 1 inch thick
Salt and pepper to taste
1/4 cup freshly coarse-ground black peppercorns
2 handfuls spring mix salad greens
1 handful baby frisée
1 bunch asparagus, lightly blanched* and shaved on a mandoline
1 cup mixed yellow and red cherry tomatoes, cut in halves
2 cups Peruvian purple potatoes, boiled, chilled, and sliced into 1/4-inch rounds
1/2 red onion, shaved thin with a mandoline
1 bunch chives, cut in 1-inch batons
1/4 cup chopped Italian parsley
1 cup truffle vinaigrette

POACHED PEAR AND ST. ANDRÉ SALAD

Serves 4

The vibrant color of the pears gives this delicate dish a regal look. Poached with red wine, cinnamon, and star anise, the fruit offers an explosion of fresh flavor. It becomes the centerpiece of a salad of mâche and baby frisée, candied pecans, warmed St. André cheese, crostini, Champagne Vinaigrette, and a drizzle of balsamic reduction. Consider it for special occasions as a first or second course, or even as a separate salad course just before you serve dessert.

What You Need

4-quart saucepan 2 baking sheets 2-quart saucepan Large bowl

How to Make

FOR THE POACHED PEARS:

1. Peel the pears, leaving the stem intact. Put them in the saucepan and add wine, sugar, cinnamon, star anise, a pinch of salt, and enough water to cover.
2. Poach* slowly over medium heat until fork-tender but not mushy, about 30 to 35 minutes.
3. Pull off heat and let cool in the liquid. Refrigerate in the liquid overnight.

FOR THE SALAD:

1. In the 2-quart saucepan, add balsamic vinegar. Reduce* over medium-low heat to 1/4 cup, about 10 to 12 minutes. Set aside to cool.
2. Preheat oven to 325F.
3. Make crostini. Brush each baguette slice with olive oil and place on baking sheet. Bake in oven until crostini are crisp and golden brown, about 10 to 12 minutes. Set aside.
4. Preheat oven to 400F.
5. Remove pears from poaching liquid and let drain. Cut a little off the bottom of the pears so that they can stand upright. With a small spoon, remove the cores through the bottom of the pears, leaving the stems intact. Stand 1 pear on each plate.
6. In the oven, warm the cheese, pecans, and crostini.
7. In the bowl, toss the mâche and frisée with the Champagne Vinaigrette, salt, and pepper.
8. Place a small pile of greens next to each pear. Put a wedge of cheese on the plate and top with a crostini sticking up like a fin.
9. Place a few pecans around the edge of each plate and drizzle a strip of balsamic reduction along one side.

Ingredients

For the poached pears:

4 Bosc or red pears
3 cups red wine (of a quality you'd like to drink, preferably a zinfandel or merlot)
1/2 cup granulated sugar
1 cinnamon stick
1 star anise
Salt

For the salad:

4 slices baguette, cut diagonally, about 5 inches long and no more than 1/4 inch thick
Olive oil
4 poached pears
2 cups mâche
1 cup torn baby frisée
1/2 cup candied pecans (see Candied Walnuts, p. 222), in large pieces
4 2-ounce wedges St. André cheese
1 cup aged balsamic vinegar
1/4 cup Champagne Vinaigrette (recipe, p. 231)
Salt and pepper to taste

*See "reduce" in the Glossary; for poaching, see Tips and Techniques.

SEARED DUCK AND BLOOD ORANGE SALAD

Serves 4

Almost everybody is familiar with the classic flavors of duck and orange. If you're not, take it from me, the combo works very well. This salad celebrates these flavors and adds highlights of fennel, Manchego cheese, candied pecans, and blood orange vinaigrette.

Blood oranges are fairly easy to find between November and February. The flesh is a purplish red, and though they're similar in flavor to a navel or Valencia orange, their sweetness seems more intense.

Please do not overcook the duck. It will have the best flavor and texture when cooked medium-rare to medium.

What You Need

12-inch frying pan that can go from stovetop to oven, such as cast iron
2 mixing bowls   Meat thermometer   Large bowl   Vegetable zester
Cooling rack

How to Make

FOR THE BLOOD ORANGE VINAIGRETTE:

In a bowl, whisk together all ingredients except the oil; then slowly drizzle in the oil while continuing to whisk rapidly. Add salt and pepper to taste.

FOR THE DUCK:

Preheat oven to 325F.
1. In a bowl, combine marinade ingredients and duck, making sure the meat is completely submerged. Cover and refrigerate overnight.
2. The next day, shake excess marinade from duck and scrape off the pieces of ginger.
3. In the frying pan over medium heat, place duck skin side down and cook slowly for about 3 to 4 minutes.
4. Place frying pan in the oven and cook duck for another 10 to 12 minutes, until it reaches an internal temperature of 115F. The fat should be rendered and the skin crisp.
5. Set duck pieces on the rack to rest. After 5 minutes, slice thinly.

Ingredients

For the blood orange vinaigrette (makes 1 cup):

1/2 cup blood orange juice
3 tablespoons champagne vinegar
1 finely chopped* shallot
1 tablespoon finely chopped ginger
1 tablespoon honey
1/3 cup olive oil
Salt and pepper

For the duck:

1 tablespoon blood orange zest
1/4 cup blood orange juice
1 tablespoon finely chopped ginger
2 tablespoons soy sauce
1 teaspoon brown sugar
1 chopped shallot
1 teaspoon olive oil
2 large duck breasts, fat trimmed and skin lightly scored in a grid pattern (ask the butcher to do this for you)

FOR THE SALAD:

1. Place 1 radicchio leaf on each of four plates, so it forms a cup.
2. In the large bowl, toss the arugula, sliced duck, oranges, and fennel with vinaigrette, salt, and pepper.
3. Place equal amounts of salad in each radicchio leaf cup.
4. With the vegetable zester, shave the Manchego cheese. Top each salad with the cheese and pecans.
5. Drizzle a little more dressing around the edge of each plate. Serve immediately.

*See "chop" in the Glossary.

Ingredients continued

For the salad:

4 radicchio leaves
4 handfuls baby arugula
Sliced duck breasts
8 blood oranges, peeled, sliced, seeds removed
1 cup finely shaved fennel, lightly salted
1/4 cup blood orange vinaigrette
Salt and pepper to taste
1 2-ounce piece Manchego cheese
1/2 cup candied pecans (see Candied Walnuts, p. 222)

GRILLED VEGETABLE SALAD WITH RICOTTA SALATA

Serves 4 to 6

I love the beauty of this vegetarian salad, which makes a festive side dish for a summer picnic. Assorted vegetables with different colors and textures are grilled, tossed with balsamic vinaigrette and fresh herbs, and finished with shaved ricotta salata, which adds creaminess and additional texture. Toss with chilled wagon-wheel pasta for a salad that's a meal in itself.

What You Need

Grill or grill pan   Large bowl

How to Make

FOR THE BALSAMIC VINAIGRETTE:

Whisk together all the ingredients except olive and canola oils; then slowly drizzle in the oils, continuing to whisk until the mixture is thick and emulsified. Add salt and pepper to taste. Set aside.

FOR THE VEGETABLE SALAD:

1. Set grill to medium-high. Combine olive oil and balsamic vinegar. Toss the zucchinis, eggplant, onion, fennel, bell pepper, mushrooms, and asparagus with this mixture, using just enough to coat.
2. Grill* vegetables until soft, turning them regularly, about 5 to 8 minutes. Set aside to cool.
3. When vegetables are cool, cut into a variety of shapes, for interest.
4. In the bowl, toss vegetables with the garlic, basil, parsley, chives, tarragon, spinach, and 1/2 cup balsamic vinaigrette.
5. Lay the salad out on a platter and top with shaved ricotta salata, basil leaves, and sprigs of parsley, chives, and tarragon.

*See "chop" in the Glossary; for grilling, see Tips and Techniques.

Ingredients

For the balsamic vinaigrette
(makes 1 cup):

1/4 cup aged balsamic vinegar
(eight-year-old is best)
1 tablespoon finely chopped*
shallots
1 teaspoon finely chopped garlic
1 tablespoon honey
1/4 cup extra-virgin olive oil
1/3 cup canola oil
Salt and pepper

Ingredients continued

For the vegetable salad:

1/3 cup olive oil

3 tablespoons balsamic vinegar

2 6-inch green zucchinis, cut in half lengthwise

2 6-inch yellow zucchinis, cut in half lengthwise

2 6-inch Japanese eggplants, cut in half lengthwise

2 thick slices red onion

1 fennel bulb, cut into 1/3-inch slices, with core intact

1 red bell pepper, quartered and seeded

2 portobello mushrooms, about 4 inches in diameter, cleaned, stems removed

8 standard asparagus, bottoms cut off

3 handfuls baby spinach leaves

1/2 teaspoon chopped garlic

2 tablespoons chopped basil leaves plus more for garnish

2 tablespoons chopped parsley plus sprigs for garnish

2 tablespoons chopped chives plus sprigs for garnish

1 tablespoon chopped tarragon plus sprigs for garnish

1/2 cup balsamic vinaigrette

4-ounce piece ricotta salata (a semi-hard ricotta cheese, available at most markets with good cheese departments)

PEPPER STEAK SALAD WITH MAYTAG BLUE CHEESE

Serves 4

Meat and potatoes are the main focus of this summertime salad, but the balsamic vinaigrette, fresh herbs, and crumbled blue cheese put a new twist on the traditional duo. I think a New York cut goes best in this recipe, but flat iron, flank, or even filet mignon will work—it just depends on your taste.

What You Need

12-inch frying pan   Whisk   Mixing bowl   Meat thermometer

How to Make

FOR THE BALSAMIC VINAIGRETTE:

Whisk together honey, balsamic vinegar, garlic, and shallots. Slowly drizzle in canola and olive oils, continuing to whisk. Add salt and pepper to taste.

FOR THE PEPPER STEAK AND SALAD:

1. Heat the frying pan over medium-high heat and add just enough olive oil to make a thin film on the pan.
2. Salt each steak and cover one side generously with coarsely ground black pepper. Pack on the seasonings.
3. Put steaks into the hot pan pepper side down and sear until edges start to brown, about 4 minutes.
4. Flip and cook the other side, another 4 minutes for medium-rare. The steaks should read 110F to 115F on a meat thermometer.
5. Pull frying pan off heat and let steaks rest for 5 minutes.
6. Set 1 radicchio leaf on each of four plates, so it forms a cup.
7. Thinly slice the steaks. Toss in a large bowl with watercress, salad greens, potatoes, tomatoes, celery, chives, thyme, onion, half the blue cheese, balsamic vinaigrette, salt, and pepper.
8. Serve salad in radicchio leaf cup, topped with a little more blue cheese and chive sprigs.

*See "chop" and "dice" in the Glossary; for cutting on the bias, see Tips and Techniques.

Ingredients

For the balsamic vinaigrette
    (makes about 3/4 cup):
1 tablespoon honey
1/4 cup aged balsamic vinegar
    (at least eight years old)
1 garlic clove, peeled and finely
    diced*
1 tablespoon finely diced shallot
1/4 cup olive oil
1/4 cup canola oil
Salt and pepper

Ingredients continued

For the pepper steak and salad:

4 8-ounce New York steaks

Olive oil

Salt to taste

1/4 cup coarsely ground black
pepper

4 whole radicchio leaves

2 bunches watercress or baby
arugula, washed and dried

2 large handfuls spring mix salad
greens

2 cups boiled and chilled fingerling potatoes, sliced
lengthwise

1 cup cherry tomato medley,
halved

2 vine-ripened tomatoes, cut
into thin wedges

1 stalk celery, sliced thin on the
bias*

1 bunch chives, chopped,* plus
sprigs for garnish

1 tablespoon chopped fresh
thyme

1/2 red onion, sliced

1/2 cup crumbled Maytag Blue
Cheese

3/4 cup balsamic vinaigrette

POACHED SALMON SALAD WITH DILL-MUSTARD DRESSING

Serves 4

Sometimes a smaller, elegant salad, served as a light summer dinner or a first course, is just what I crave: a salad like this one. The velvety dressing that tops the salmon is enlivened with lemon, mustard, and dill. The rest of the salad is tossed lightly with olive oil and lemon to keep the flavors fresh and alive.

What You Need

Food processor   12-inch frying pan   Slotted spatula and spoon
Large bowl   Plastic squeeze bottle

How to Make

FOR THE DILL-MUSTARD DRESSING:

1. In the food processor, blend lemon juice, White Wine Worcestershire sauce, vinegar, egg yolks, shallots, honey, and mustard.
2. Mix well; then slowly drizzle in the oil. The dressing should become fairly thick.
3. Add salt and pepper.
4. Turn off food processor and add chopped dill to the dressing.
5. Put the dressing into a squeeze bottle.

FOR THE SALMON:

1. In the frying pan, heat the wine, water, clam juice, vinegar, and bay leaf. Let simmer* over medium heat for 4 to 5 minutes.
2. Put 1 slice of lemon on top of each piece of salmon. Place salmon in liquid, cover, and poach* over medium heat for about 5 minutes.
3. Remove fish with the slotted spatula. Discard the lemon and season fish with olive oil, salt, and pepper.
4. Skim salmon fat from poaching liquid.

Ingredients

For the dill-mustard dressing
 (makes a little more than 1 cup):

1/4 cup lemon juice
1 tablespoon White Wine Worcestershire sauce*
2 tablespoons champagne vinegar
2 coddled* egg yolks
2 tablespoons chopped* shallots
1 tablespoon honey
2 tablespoons Dijon mustard
4 tablespoons extra-virgin olive oil
3/4 cup canola oil
Salt and pepper to taste
1/4 cup chopped fresh dill

For the salmon:

1/2 cup white wine (of a quality you'd like to drink)
1/2 cup water
1/4 cup clam juice
1 teaspoon champagne vinegar
1 bay leaf
1 lemon
4 5-ounce salmon fillets
2 tablespoons extra-virgin olive oil
Salt and pepper to taste

FOR THE SALAD:

1. Crack eggs into the salmon poaching liquid and poach over medium heat until medium-firm, about 3 to 4 minutes.
2. While eggs are poaching, toss the frisée, tomatoes, red onion, green beans, potatoes, asparagus, parsley, dill, and chives in the bowl with olive oil, lemon juice, salt, and pepper. Remove asparagus and set aside.
3. Divide salad equally among four plates, retaining a little frisée, and lay 2 asparagus spears on top.
4. Lay salmon on top of the asparagus. Try to tuck all ingredients underneath each piece of fish.
5. With the slotted spoon, take out the poached eggs and set one on each serving of salmon and salad.
6. With the squeeze bottle, drizzle the dill-mustard dressing across the whole plate. Then put a little frisée and a couple of chive sprigs on top of the egg. Serve immediately.

*See "chop," "dice," "simmer," and "White Wine Worcestershire sauce" in the Glossary; for blanching, coddling, and poaching, see Tips and Techniques.

Ingredients continued

For the salad:

4 extra-large eggs
3 cups baby frisée
1 cup cherry tomatoes, finely diced*
1/4 cup finely diced red onion
1-1/2 cups blanched* French green beans
1 cup boiled baby red potatoes, sliced thin
8 spears blanched and peeled asparagus
2 tablespoons chopped Italian parsley
2 tablespoons chopped fresh dill
2 tablespoons chopped chives plus sprigs for garnish
4 tablespoons extra-virgin olive oil
Juice of 2 lemons
Salt and pepper to taste
4 poached salmon fillets
Dill-mustard dressing

APPETIZERS

APPETIZERS

Appetizers are delicious treats meant to tease and whet your appetite for the rest of the meal. Since it is the first course, a good appetizer should be impressive, yet not too heavy. You want to leave your guests wanting more. Here you'll find recipes for tempting tidbits both hot and cold.

HOISIN SHORT RIBS

Serves 4 to 6

Spicy yet sweet, tender as a pillow, these boneless beef tidbits are a special treat that works well as either an appetizer or a main dish. They're not hard to make, but they take a little time to prepare. Serve with sweet-and-sour pickled cucumbers, and you will impress your guests. I use boneless chuck flat steak, but cross-cut short ribs will work, too.

What You Need

9 x 13-inch deep roasting pan or Dutch oven   12-inch frying pan

How to Make

Preheat oven to 400F.

1. Season ribs with five-spice powder, salt, and pepper.
2. Place the roasting pan over medium-high heat and add a little canola oil. Brown ribs on all sides, about 2-1/2 minutes per side.
3. Add ginger and garlic.
4. Set the browned meat on top and add water, vinegar, soy sauce, and bay leaf.
5. Cover with foil and bake for 3-1/2 hours or until fork tender.
6. Take the ribs out of the oven, let cool, and then refrigerate overnight in the same pan, uncovered, with all the liquid. The next day, when they are easier to work with, cut them into 1/2-inch slices.
7. Combine cucumber slices, rice vinegar, red onion, salt, and sugar. Mix well and let sit for about 15 minutes.
8. Dust the chilled ribs lightly with cornstarch.
9. In the frying pan, heat a little oil over medium-high heat and fry rib pieces on both sides until brown and crispy.
10. Drain the remaining oil; then glaze the ribs with Hoisin Sauce.
11. Set on a plate and garnish with pickled cucumbers, toasted sesame seeds, and shredded green onion.

*See "chop" in the Glossary; for toasting, see Tips and Techniques.

Ingredients

3 pounds boneless chuck flat steak
3 tablespoons Chinese five-spice powder
Salt and pepper to taste
1/4 cup canola oil plus more for cooking
1 cup roughly chopped* fresh ginger
10 garlic cloves, peeled
4 cups water
1 cup seasoned rice vinegar
1/2 cup light soy sauce
1 bay leaf
Cornstarch
2 cups Hoisin Sauce (recipe, p. 233)
1 English cucumber, peeled (leave strips of the skin, so it alternates white and green), seeded, and sliced into moons about 1/4 inch thick
1/4 cup seasoned rice vinegar
1/4 cup thinly sliced red onion
1 teaspoon salt
1 tablespoon granulated sugar
Toasted* sesame seeds
Shredded green onion, white and green parts

SWEET CHILI PORK RIBLETS

Serves 4 to 6

Want a zesty, meaty appetizer that's easy to make? Try sweet chili pork riblets — braised baby back ribs with ginger and lemongrass stir-fried in a sweet-spicy glaze. I think they're finger-licking good.

What You Need

Deep roasting pan large enough to hold 2 2-1/2-pound racks of ribs
Food processor or standing blender   12-inch frying pan or wok   Sheet pan

How to Make

FOR THE GLAZE:

In the food processor, mix all ingredients well. Refrigerate until needed.

FOR THE RIBS:

Preheat oven to 375F.

1. Rub ribs with five-spice powder, salt, and pepper.
2. Place in the roasting pan with ginger, lemongrass, garlic, vinegar, cinnamon stick, and water. Put in the oven and braise for 2 hours.
3. Remove from oven and let cool for at least 1-1/2 hours before trying to take the ribs out of the pan. Be careful that they don't fall apart. Refrigerate overnight.
4. The next day, slice them along the bones into meaty riblets.
5. Preheat broiler. In the frying pan, heat sesame and canola oils over medium heat until they just begin to smoke.
6. Lightly coat the ribs with cornstarch. Stir-fry the ribs until crisp, about 6 to 7 minutes.
7. Drain oil from frying pan and toss ribs with the glaze.
8. In the same pan, simmer* ribs with the glaze for about a minute; then spread them out on a sheet pan and set under the broiler until caramelized. They should be under the broiler for only a minute; keep an eye on them so they don't burn.
9. Place on a serving platter and garnish with green onion flowers or cilantro sprigs and orange slices. Serve hot.

*See "chop," "simmer," and "smash" in the Glossary.

Ingredients

For the glaze (makes 2 cups):

1/2 cup Thai sweet chili sauce (available in Asian markets)
1/2 cup ketchup
1/2 cup pineapple juice
1/4 cup rice vinegar
1/2 cup orange marmalade
1/2 cup light soy sauce
2 tablespoons chopped* fresh ginger
1 tablespoon chopped garlic

For the ribs:

2 racks of baby back ribs, about 2-1/2 pounds each
2 tablespoons Chinese five-spice powder
Salt and pepper to taste
1/2 cup chopped fresh ginger
2 lemongrass stalks
6 cloves garlic, peeled and smashed*
1/2 cup rice vinegar
1 cinnamon stick
3 cups water
4 tablespoons sesame oil
5 tablespoons canola oil
1/2 cup cornstarch
2 cups glaze
Green onion flowers or cilantro sprigs and orange slices

SMOKED CHICKEN WINGS

Serves 6 to 10 as an appetizer

These are a little different from typical hot wings, spicy and sweet, with a nice smoky flavor. It's hard to stop eating them. There are a couple of steps to making these wings, but you can easily spread the work out over two days. On the first day, marinate the wings. On the second day, smoke them and then serve them. Pair them with Jicama-Apple Coleslaw (recipe, p. 186) and your favorite buttermilk dressing.

What You Need

2 large bowls   Standing blender   Mixing bowl   Barbecue   10-inch saucepan
12-inch frying pan   1 pound applewood chips   Pan for wood chips

How to Make

FOR THE WING SAUCE:

In the blender, purée everything well. Transfer to the mixing bowl and store, covered, in the refrigerator until needed.

FOR THE WINGS:

1. In a large bowl, mix the drumettes well with the garlic and onion powders, cumin, cayenne pepper, sugar, red wine vinegar, and orange juice. Make sure chicken is completely submerged in the marinade. Cover the bowl and refrigerate overnight.
2. Salt and pepper the drumettes and then place the coals to one side of the barbecue. When the coals are glowing but no longer flaming, heat the pan for the wood chips, place the chips in the pan, and as the chips begin to smoke and get hot, place the chicken wings on the opposite side of the grill.
3. Cover the barbecue, leaving only a small vent open, and cook for about 10 minutes.
4. Turn and rotate the wings, cover the barbecue again, and continue to cook for another 15 minutes.
5. Preheat broiler.
6. In the saucepan, warm up the wing sauce.
7. Transfer the wings from the barbecue to a large bowl and toss with 1 cup of sauce. Then broil the wings in the oven for about 4 minutes or until caramelized.
8. Heat the rest of the sauce in the frying pan with the butter and then toss the broiled wings in the sauce with a squeeze of fresh lime. Serve immediately.

*See "Cholula hot sauce" and "smash" in the Glossary.

Ingredients

For the wing sauce (makes about 2 cups):

1 cup Cholula* or your favorite hot sauce
1/2 cup honey
1 to 2 chipotle chiles, depending on how spicy you like it
1/2 teaspoon ground cumin
3 cloves garlic, peeled and smashed*
1/2 cup ketchup
1/2 cup orange juice
1/4 cup red wine vinegar
Juice of 1 lime

For the wings:

5 pounds chicken drumettes (nice plump ones)
2 tablespoons garlic powder
2 tablespoons onion powder
1 tablespoon ground cumin
1 tablespoon cayenne pepper
1/2 cup granulated sugar
1/4 cup red wine vinegar
1/2 cup orange juice
Salt and pepper to taste
2 cups wing sauce
2 tablespoons unsalted butter
Fresh lime juice

SMOKED SALMON AND GRIDDLED CORN CAKES

Serves 4

Layers of sweet corn cakes, smoked salmon, and cucumber cream make a beautiful, elegant appetizer or brunch entrée. This dish is both light and delicious. Best of all, it's easy to make.

What You Need

Griddle   2 mixing bowls   Whisk   1-ounce ladle

How to Make

FOR THE CUCUMBER CREAM:

In a bowl, combine all ingredients and mix well. Refrigerate.

FOR THE SMOKED SALMON AND CORN CAKES:

1. In a bowl, mix corn, dill, chives, and red onion into the Basic Pancakes batter with the whisk until it has a thick, lumpy consistency.
2. Heat the griddle over medium heat and rub generously with olive oil.
3. Using a 1-ounce ladle, spoon the batter onto the griddle.
4. Cook cakes until golden brown on one side, about 4 minutes; then flip and cook until golden on the other side.
5. Place a corn cake on each of four plates and top with a slice of salmon and a dollop of cucumber cream.
6. Place a second corn cake on top, followed by another slice of salmon, a dollop of cucumber cream, and a sprig of dill.
7. Repeat layering process for each serving. Serve immediately.

*See "chop" and "dice" in the Glossary.

Ingredients

For the cucumber cream:

1/4 cup plain yogurt
1/4 cup sour cream
1/4 cup peeled, seeded, and diced* cucumber
1/4 teaspoon celery salt
2 teaspoons lemon juice
2 tablespoons chopped fresh dill
Salt and pepper to taste

For the corn cakes:

1 cup sweet corn kernels, fresh or frozen
2 tablespoons chopped* fresh dill plus 4 sprigs for garnish
2 tablespoons chopped chives
1 cup Basic Pancakes batter (recipe, p. 6)
1/4 cup finely diced red onion
Olive oil
4 slices smoked salmon, cut in half

MUSSELS WITH GREEN COCONUT CURRY SAUCE

Serves 4

These mussels shine thanks to the fresh flavors of coconut milk, cilantro, green onion, and complex green Thai curry. The combination of ingredients complements the sweet ocean brine of the shellfish. Black mussels are the best variety for this dish because they are the smallest and sweetest. Serve as an appetizer or on top of soba noodles as a main dish.

What You Need

Standing blender   12-inch frying pan with lid   2-quart saucepan

How to Make

FOR THE GREEN COCONUT CURRY SAUCE:

In the blender, purée all ingredients until smooth.

FOR THE MUSSELS:

1. Heat curry sauce in the saucepan over medium heat, being sure to stir occasionally, and reduce* until it becomes vibrant in color and slightly thicker, about 10 minutes.
2. Heat the frying pan over medium-high heat and add sesame oil.
3. When it starts to smoke, add garlic and ginger and sauté* for 10 seconds. Then add the mussels with a pinch of salt and pepper and toss together. Let sit for a couple of seconds.
4. Add the curry sauce to the mussels and cover the pan so the steam will help force the mussels open.
5. When the mussels are opened, remove from sauce and place in a serving bowl.
6. Reduce the sauce again over medium-high heat until it's slightly thick (the consistency of heavy cream), about 2 to 3 more minutes. Pour over the mussels. Top with a squeeze of lime and the chopped cilantro, basil, and mint. Garnish with cilantro sprigs.

*See "chop," "dice," "reduce," "sauté," and "Thai curry paste" in the Glossary; for cleaning mussels, see Tips and Techniques.

Ingredients

For the green coconut curry sauce (makes 2-1/2 cups):

1/4 cup red bell pepper, diced*
1/4 cup green bell pepper, diced
1/2 cup chopped* cilantro
1/4 chopped fresh basil
1/4 cup chopped fresh mint
1/2 cup clam juice
1 tablespoon green Thai curry paste* (for a spicier profile, add more to taste)
2 cups canned unsweetened coconut milk
1 tablespoon sesame oil
3 tablespoons chopped ginger
2 tablespoons chopped garlic
1/2 cup chopped green onion, white and green parts

For the mussels:

2 cups green coconut curry sauce
2 tablespoons sesame oil
1 tablespoon chopped garlic
1 tablespoon finely chopped ginger
30 black mussels, cleaned* and bearded
Salt and pepper
Lime juice
1/4 cup chopped cilantro plus sprigs for garnish
1/4 cup chopped fresh basil
1/4 cup chopped fresh mint

BAKED OYSTERS WITH BACON TRUFFLE BUTTER

Serves 4

What makes this dish sparkle is the sweet ocean flavor of the oysters contrasted with the earthy, smoky taste of the bacon and truffles. Bluepoint oysters work well with this dish because they are large enough to make a generous mouthful but not so large that their sweetness disappears. If you make the truffle butter ahead of time, you can prepare this dish very quickly. Simply shuck the oysters, top with the butter, broil them, and enjoy.

What You Need

Cookie sheet   Small mixing bowl   2 cups rock salt for presentation

How to Make

FOR THE TRUFFLE BUTTER:

1. Soften butter to room temperature. Mix well with all the other ingredients.
2. Spoon the mass of seasoned butter onto a piece of wax paper. Rolling the paper around the butter and working it with your hands, shape it into a tight roll about the circumference of a half dollar. Refrigerate until the seasoned butter hardens.

FOR THE OYSTERS:

1. Preheat the broiler.
2. On the cookie sheet, line up the shucked oysters on the half shell. Make sure they are level so that the butter won't spill out when it melts.
3. Slice disks of butter about 1/4-inch thick and top each oyster with one disk.
4. Sprinkle about 1 teaspoon of Parmesan on each.
5. Place oysters under the broiler and, watching carefully, cook until they are browned and bubbling around the edges.
6. Mound rock salt on a platter. Place the broiled oysters in their shells on top of the salt, garnish with chopped parsley and lemon wedges, and serve immediately.

(Note: If you have any leftover seasoned butter, it can be stored in the freezer for up to 2 months.)

*See "chop" and "Parmesan" in the Glossary.

Ingredients

For the truffle butter:

1/2 pound (2 sticks) unsalted butter
2 tablespoons chopped* garlic
2 tablespoons chopped shallots
1/4 cup cooked, chopped bacon
3 tablespoons truffle oil
3 tablespoons chopped parsley
3 tablespoons chopped green onion, both white and green parts
Salt and pepper to taste
3 tablespoons lemon juice

For the oysters:

16 shucked bluepoint oysters, rinsed and with the muscle detached
Truffle butter
1/2 cup grated Parmesan*
1/4 cup chopped parsley
Lemon wedges

AHI TUNA TARTARE WITH LEMONGRASS ON WONTON CRISPS

Serves 4

Fresh ahi tuna served on crackly-crunchy wonton crisps with diced cucumber, papaya, cilantro, serrano chile, and red onion makes for beautiful tidbits with a hint of spice. Tangy lemongrass flavor enlivens the fish, thanks to this exciting dressing.

What You Need

Small saucepan   Blender   Container for chilling sauce   Strainer
Deep-fryer or 12-inch deep-sided skillet and cooking thermometer
Tongs   Large plate   Large bowl

How to Make

FOR THE DRESSING:

1. Put lemongrass, ginger, garlic, rice vinegar, sherry, bay leaf, and jalapeño chile in a small saucepan and bring to a boil.
2. Remove from heat, let cool, pour into the container, and refrigerate overnight.
3. The next day, strain, pour into the blender, and add honey, soy sauce, and sesame oil. Blend for 30 seconds.

FOR THE TUNA TARTARE AND WONTON CRISPS:

1. Line the large plate with paper towels.
2. Heat deep-fryer or Crisco to 350F.
3. Place wonton wrappers one by one into the hot oil. Make sure they are flat, not folded, and don't overlap.
4. Let cook until the edges are light brown; then turn them over with the tongs and let cook a few more seconds. Remove with tongs and lay on the paper-towel-lined plate to drain.
5. In the large bowl, toss the tuna with the ginger, serrano chile, papaya, cucumber, sesame seeds, red onion, and cilantro.
6. Add 1/3 cup dressing to the tuna mixture and toss gently with a spoon. There should be only just enough dressing to lightly coat the mixture. Salt and pepper to taste.
7. Place a heaping spoonful of tuna tartare on each wonton crisp and serve immediately.

*See "chop," "dice," and "smash" in the Glossary; for toasting, see Tips and Techniques.

Ingredients

For the dressing:

1 stalk fresh lemongrass, chopped* fine
1/4 cup finely chopped fresh ginger
3 cloves garlic, smashed*
1/4 cup seasoned rice vinegar
1/3 cup sherry
1 bay leaf
1/2 jalapeño chile, cut in half
2 teaspoons honey
1/2 cup soy sauce
3 tablespoons sesame oil

For the tuna tartare and wonton crisps:

15 to 18 wonton wrappers
2 cups Crisco or vegetable oil
1 cup fresh sushi-grade ahi tuna (about 8 ounces, cut into 1/4-inch dice)
1 teaspoon finely chopped fresh ginger
1 teaspoon seeded, finely diced* serrano chile
1/2 cup diced ripe papaya (cut into 1/4-inch dice)
1/2 cup peeled, seeded, diced cucumber (cut into 1/4-inch dice)
1 teaspoon sesame seeds, toasted*
1/4 cup finely diced red onion
1/4 cup chopped cilantro
1/3 cup dressing
Salt and pepper

STUFFED CALAMARI

Serves 4 to 6

This unusual appetizer takes a little extra time to prepare, but the results are beautiful and professional-looking. The calamari is stuffed with pancetta, crab, onions, fennel, herbs, and bread crumbs and then fried, sliced, and served with a tomato-Pernod sauce. A deep-fryer works best with this recipe.

What You Need

10-inch frying pan   2-quart saucepan   Whisk   Toothpicks   Rack
Deep-fryer or 12-inch deep-sided skillet and cooking thermometer

How to Make

FOR THE STUFFING:

1. In the frying pan, melt butter over medium-high heat and sauté* pancetta until almost cooked, about 3 minutes.
2. Add celery, onions, fennel, bay leaf, and garlic. Cook until translucent, about 5 more minutes.
3. Add white wine and clam juice and reduce* by half, about 3 minutes. Remove bay leaf.
4. Add Croutons and mix well until all liquid is absorbed and the mixture has the consistency of moist stuffing.
5. Place in a bowl and add crabmeat, basil, parsley, and salt and pepper to taste. Let cool and refrigerate overnight.

FOR THE TOMATO-PERNOD SAUCE:

1. In the saucepan over medium-high heat, reduce wine, clam juice, tomatoes, cream, shallots, garlic, and Pernod for about 10 to 15 minutes. The sauce should have the consistency of thick cream.
2. Remove from heat, whisk in the butter, and add dill, parsley, lemon juice, salt, and pepper.

Ingredients

For the stuffing:

3 tablespoons unsalted butter
1/2 cup chopped* pancetta
1/2 cup finely diced* celery
1/2 cup finely diced yellow onions
1/2 cup finely diced fennel bulb
1 bay leaf
1/2 tablespoon chopped garlic
1/4 cup dry white wine (of a quality you'd like to drink)
1/2 cup clam juice
1-1/2 cups Croutons (see Crostini and Croutons, p. 224)
1 cup Dungeness crabmeat
2 tablespoons chopped fresh basil
2 tablespoons chopped Italian parsley
Salt and pepper

For the tomato-Pernod sauce (makes 1 cup):

1 cup dry white wine (of a quality you'd like to drink)
1/2 cup clam juice
1/2 cup diced fresh or canned tomatoes
1/2 cup heavy cream
3 tablespoons finely diced shallots
1/2 teaspoon chopped garlic
2 ounces Pernod
5 tablespoons unsalted butter

FOR THE CALAMARI:

1. Clean calamari tubes by putting your fingers inside each tube and feeling for any cartilage. Pull out the cartilage with your fingers so that the inside of each tube is smooth. Rinse and pat dry on paper towels.
2. Fill calamari tubes with the stuffing, which should be moist, not too wet or too dry.
3. Hold the ends of each tube together with two toothpicks.
4. Mix 1 cup flour, salt, pepper, paprika, and garlic and onion powders.
5. Pour oil into the deep-fryer to a depth of 1/2 inch and heat to 350F.
6. Dip the stuffed calamari tubes in plain flour, then in buttermilk, and then in the seasoned flour mixture. Be sure they are well coated. Let sit for 15 minutes.
7. Lay the tubes gently in the hot oil and fry* on both sides until golden brown, about 3 minutes per side.
8. Remove to a rack to dry.
9. Remove the black center of each tentacle, rinse, and pat dry. Coat tentacles well with seasoned flour and fry in the oil for about 4 minutes, until crisp and golden brown.
10. Remove to a towel to drain.
11. Slice each calamari tube in half and arrange on a plate.
12. Spoon some of the tomato-Pernod sauce over and around the calamari tubes and top with the fried tentacles.
13. Squeeze a little lemon juice over all and garnish with dill. Serve immediately.

*See "chop," "dice," "reduce," and "sauté" in the Glossary; for frying, see Tips and Techniques.

Ingredients continued

2 tablespoons chopped fresh dill
2 tablespoons chopped parsley
2 tablespoons lemon juice
Salt and pepper to taste

For the calamari:

18 3-inch calamari tubes, cleaned
Calamari tentacles
Stuffing
1 cup flour plus more for coating
1 teaspoon salt
1/2 teaspoon pepper
1/2 teaspoon paprika
2 tablespoons garlic powder
2 tablespoons onion powder
2 cups Crisco or vegetable oil
1/2 cup buttermilk
Tomato-Pernod sauce
Lemon juice
Fresh dill

ROCK SHRIMP COCKTAIL

Makes 4 cocktails

There's south-of-the-border flair in this spicy, refreshing shrimp cocktail. Mango, avocado, cilantro, and fresh tomato add colorful, flavorful twists. Rock shrimp are an excellent choice because they're particularly tender and sweet, but you can use other shrimp, too. Think about mixing fresh Dungeness crabmeat into the cocktail as well.

What You Need

2-quart saucepan   Sheet pan   Mixing bowl   4 8-ounce martini glasses for presentation

How to Make

FOR THE COCKTAIL SAUCE:

Mix all ingredients together.

FOR THE ROCK SHRIMP COCKTAIL:

1. Bring saucepan of water to a boil over medium-high heat.
2. Add lemon halves, salt to taste, and pickling spices. Let simmer* for 15 minutes; then add shrimp and cook for about 3 minutes.
3. Lay shrimp out on sheet pan and refrigerate for 1 hour, until chilled.
4. In the bowl, mix chilled rock shrimp, avocado, mango, chopped cilantro, mint, red onion, tomatoes, cucumber, jalapeño chile, cocktail sauce, lime juice, dash of Tabasco sauce, salt, and pepper and toss gently.
5. Place a little shredded lettuce in the bottom of each martini glass and top with the shrimp mixture. Garnish each cocktail with a tortilla chip sticking up, cilantro sprigs, and a lime wedge pushed onto the rim of the glass.

*See "chop," "Cholula hot sauce," "dice," and "simmer" in the Glossary.

Ingredients

For the cocktail sauce (makes 1 cup):

1/2 cup ketchup
2 tablespoons tomato paste
1/3 cup V-8 juice
2 tablespoons Cholula* or your favorite hot sauce
1 teaspoon horseradish
1 tablespoon Worcestershire sauce
1/2 teaspoon chili powder
1/4 teaspoon ground cumin
1/4 teaspoon celery salt
2 tablespoons lime juice

Ingredients continued

For the rock shrimp cocktail:

1 lemon, cut in half
1 tablespoon pickling spices
2 cups raw rock shrimp
2 avocados, diced*
1 cup diced mango
1/2 cup chopped* cilantro
2 tablespoons chopped mint
1/2 cup finely diced red onion
1/2 cup peeled, diced tomatoes
1/2 cup cucumber, peeled,
    seeded, and diced
2 tablespoons finely diced
    jalapeño chile
3/4 cup cocktail sauce
Juice of 2 limes
Tabasco sauce
Salt and pepper
1-1/2 cups shredded romaine
    lettuce
4 tortilla chips
Cilantro sprigs
4 lime wedges

ENTRÉES

ENTRÉES

The entrée is the centerpiece of your lunch or dinner. It should be fulfilling to your senses in terms of how it looks, tastes, and smells. Most of the recipes in this chapter are simple, but I've included some that are a little more challenging. This is to encourage you to develop your skills, not only in following the recipes but also in creating your own. Change some of the flavors in your sauces. Mix and match sides. Try different seasonings. Learn to smell as you cook so you'll be able to really appreciate what you're doing. The more you engage all your senses in the process, the more you'll truly develop as a cook.

GRILLED HOISIN CHICKEN

Serves 4 to 6

This is an Asian-inspired way to barbecue chicken and load it up with flavor. Serve with steamed rice and baby bok choy with ginger and garlic for a complete meal.

What You Need

Mixing bowl   Grill   Pastry brush

How to Make

1. In the mixing bowl, combine chicken with ginger, garlic, sambal, soy sauce, brown sugar, green onion, sherry, sesame and canola oils, and jalapeño chile. Mix well.
2. Cut 1 orange into quarters. Squeeze out the juice, and then add both juice and rinds to the chicken and marinade. Cover and refrigerate overnight.
3. When ready to cook, heat the grill and spray it with PAM cooking spray. Grill* chicken over medium heat for about 8 minutes, making sure it doesn't burn; then turn over and cook for another 8 minutes, constantly rotating the chicken so that the pieces don't burn.
4. When chicken is almost finished, brush Hoisin Sauce over each piece. Continue to cook, carefully watching the surface, which should quickly caramelize. Make sure the chicken doesn't burn. As the pieces become deeply browned, move them to the edge of the grill and let the sauce bake in for a few minutes. Keep brushing on sauce until chicken is done, about 4 more minutes; then give the pieces one last good coating of sauce.
5. Pull chicken off grill, place on a platter, and sprinkle with sesame seeds. Cut remaining 2 oranges into wedges. Garnish the chicken with orange wedges and cilantro sprigs.

*See "chop," "PAM cooking spray," and "sambal" in the Glossary; for grilling and toasting, see Tips and Techniques.

Ingredients

2 2-1/2-pound chickens, each cut into 8 pieces
2 tablespoons chopped* fresh ginger
2 tablespoons chopped garlic
1 tablespoon sambal*
1/4 cup light soy sauce
2 tablespoons brown sugar
1/2 cup finely chopped green onion, both white and green parts
1/4 cup dry sherry
2 tablespoons sesame oil
3 tablespoons canola oil
1 jalapeño chile, cut in half
3 oranges
PAM cooking spray*
1-1/2 cups Hoisin Sauce (recipe, p. 233)
Lightly toasted* sesame seeds
Cilantro sprigs

WHISKEY PEPPER STEAK

Serves 4

I love steak, and this is one of my favorite ways to prepare it. The recipe pays homage to the elegant dish Steak Diane, in which filet mignon medallions are sautéed with cognac and shallots. In this version, I introduce stronger flavors with the pepper crust, rich Basic Demi-glace, and a good-quality bourbon.

   I recommend New York steak here because it has enough flavor to stand up to the sauce, plus it's a juicy cut. Serve the steaks with Potato Croquettes (recipe, p. 195) and grilled asparagus dressed with lemon and olive oil.

What You Need

12-inch ovenproof frying pan, such as cast iron   Meat thermometer

How to Make

Preheat oven to 400F.
1. Rub steaks with 2 tablespoons of olive oil and the thyme and season with salt. Pack the cracked pepper generously on one side of each steak.
2. Heat frying pan over medium-high heat and add the remaining 2 tablespoons of olive oil. When it begins to smoke, lay in steaks, pepper side down. When steaks are nicely browned on one side and the pepper is crisp, about 4 to 5 minutes, flip steaks, remove frying pan from heat, and drain any excess oil.
3. Place frying pan with steaks in the oven for about 7 minutes. Check the meat to be sure it does not overcook. Insert the meat thermometer into the thickest part of each steak. When the steaks are rare, about 105F to 110F, pull the frying pan out of the oven and return to the stovetop.
4. Over medium heat, add shallots and deglaze* the pan with the bourbon. The liquor will ignite, so stand back.
5. When the flames die down, add the Basic Demi-glace. If demi-glace is too thick, dilute with a little water. Simmer* for a few seconds. When the sauce begins to thicken, add the butter and a little salt — remember, you already have enough pepper.
6. At this point, the meat should be medium-rare, between 110F and 120F on the meat thermometer. If you prefer your meat more well-done, leave it in the oven longer.
7. Place a steak on each of four plates and pour sauce on top. Serve immediately.

*See "chop," "deglaze," and "simmer" in the Glossary.

Ingredients

4 10-ounce New York steaks
4 tablespoons olive oil
2 tablespoons chopped* fresh thyme
1/3 cup freshly cracked black peppercorns
3 tablespoons chopped shallots
3/4 cup Basic Demi-glace (recipe, p. 228), heated
2 ounces good-quality bourbon
2 tablespoons unsalted butter
Salt to taste

(Note: If you don't have the time to make the demi-glace yourself, many butchers in higher-end markets sell prepared demi-glace.)

POMEGRANATE PORK CHOPS

Serves 4

Consider this dish for the holidays — or any autumn or winter day when you're in the mood for a savory-sweet meal. The pork is caramelized with a tangy pomegranate-balsamic glaze. I like to serve it on roasted butternut squash purée, topped with pomegranate seeds and fried sage and squash. Green beans are a delicious side dish and balance the richness of the pork.

What You Need

3-quart covered container for brining   Mixing bowl   Whisk   Grill
2-quart saucepan   9 x 13-inch baking dish   10-inch frying pan
Vegetable peeler   Cooking thermometer

How to Make

1. In the container, put in the chops and add 1 quart of water, champagne vinegar, onion, celery, pickling spices, cinnamon sticks, 1/3 cup sugar, and 3 tablespoons salt. Mix well and refrigerate overnight.

2. Preheat oven to 375F. With the vegetable peeler, make 1 cup of squash strips. Rub olive oil on squash halves and then salt and pepper them. Place in baking dish, cover dish with foil, and roast for about 1 hour or until fork-tender.

3. Scoop out squash flesh and place in a mixing bowl. Mix in butter, brown sugar, cream, salt, and pepper. With a whisk, mash and whip well. Set aside.

4. When ready to cook the pork chops, in the saucepan over medium-high heat, reduce* the pomegranate juice, bay leaf, balsamic vinegar, red wine, and 3 tablespoons sugar until the liquid develops the consistency of a light syrup, about 15 to 20 minutes. Set aside until needed for the pork chops.

5. Remove pork chops from marinade and pat dry. Toss with a little olive oil, salt, and pepper and grill* over medium-high heat until medium-rare, about 7 to 8 minutes per side.

6. Brush the chops generously with the pomegranate-balsamic glaze, reserving a little to drizzle on the finished plates. Place chops under the broiler for about 3 to 5 minutes, checking often so they don't burn. The glaze should become caramelized, and the pork should be about medium. Remove from broiler and keep warm.

7. In the frying pan, melt butter and sauté* the shallots. Then add green beans and 1/4 cup water. Cook over medium heat until the water evaporates, about 5 to 7 minutes. Salt and pepper to taste.

8. In the frying pan, heat Crisco over medium heat to around 325F. Add squash strips and sage in one layer.

9. Fry* until both strips and leaves are crispy but only lightly browned, about 4 minutes. (If the color becomes too dark, the oil is too hot.) Remove from pan, drain on a paper towel, and season with salt.

10. Reheat the mashed squash.

11. Put 1/2 cup of mashed squash in the center of each of four plates. Place a pork chop on top. Arrange green beans around the center and drizzle everything with a little glaze. Top with pomegranate seeds and fried squash and sage. Serve immediately.

*See "chop," "dice," "reduce," and "sauté" in the Glossary; for blanching, frying, and grilling, see Tips and Techniques.

Ingredients

4 10-ounce boneless center-cut pork chops

1 quart plus 1/4 cup water

1/4 cup champagne vinegar

1 yellow onion, roughly chopped*

2 celery stalks, roughly chopped

2 tablespoons pickling spices

2 cinnamon sticks

1/3 cup plus 3 tablespoons granulated sugar

3 tablespoons salt plus more to taste

1 large or 2 small butternut squash, halved

4 tablespoons olive oil

Pepper to taste

3 tablespoons butter

2 tablespoons brown sugar

1/4 cup cream

1 cup 100% pomegranate juice

1 bay leaf

1/2 cup eight-year-old balsamic vinegar

1/2 cup red wine (of a quality you'd like to drink)

Olive oil

5 tablespoons unsalted butter

2 tablespoons finely diced* shallots

2 cups blanched* French green beans

1/4 cup Crisco

8 fresh sage leaves

3/4 cup cleaned pomegranate seeds

BRAISED DUCK AND PORCINI PAPPARDELLE

Serves 4 to 6

Braising is one of my favorite techniques because the slow-cooking process infuses ingredients with deep, intense flavors. In this recipe, the earthy nuances of the porcini play off the dusky richness of the duck and the silkiness of the wide noodles.

I've been making this dish for many years and still enjoy it as much today as the first time I made it. You can break up the preparation time by braising and shredding the duck the day before you finish the sauce and serve the noodles.

What You Need

Coffee filter or cheesecloth   Butcher string   12-inch frying pan   Sheet pan
Deep roasting or braising pan   4-quart saucepan   Pasta pot

How to Make

FOR THE DUCK:

Preheat oven to 375F.

1. Put cinnamon stick, star anise, bay leaf, and peppercorns in a coffee filter and tie it off with butcher string.
2. Salt and pepper the duck legs and brown on both sides in the frying pan, about 4 minutes per side. Set the browned duck legs in the roasting pan.
3. Deglaze* the frying pan with a little wine and scrape the contents into the roasting pan. Add the rest of the wine, beef stock, tomato paste, tomatoes, shallots, onion, garlic, porcini, and the coffee filter containing the spices.
4. Cover the roasting pan and bake for 2-1/2 hours.
5. Remove the roasting pan from the oven, lift out the duck legs, and set them on the sheet pan to cool.
6. Carefully shred the meat off the bones, making sure there are no bits of bone in the meat. Mix the shredded duck with the braising liquid.
7. Remove the coffee filter containing the spices and pour the duck and braising liquid into the saucepan. The mixture should look fairly thick. If it's not thick enough, simmer* gently over low heat until reduced* to a stewlike consistency.

Ingredients

For the duck:

1 cinnamon stick

1 star anise

1 bay leaf

1 tablespoon whole black peppercorns

5 duck legs, skin trimmed off (ask the butcher to do this for you)

Salt and pepper to taste

2 cups red wine (of a quality you'd like to drink)

4 cups beef stock

3 tablespoons tomato paste

2 cups chopped fresh tomatoes

3 tablespoons chopped* shallots

1/2 yellow onion, finely chopped

2 tablespoons smashed* garlic

4 ounces dried porcini mushrooms

FOR THE SAUCE AND PAPPARDELLE:

1. Fill the pasta pot with water and bring to a boil.
2. In the frying pan, add half the butter and sauté* the chopped garlic until it softens; then add the braised duck mixture and marinara sauce and bring to a simmer.
3. Add plenty of salt to the boiling water in the pasta pot. Add pasta and cook for about 3 minutes at a rapid boil if using fresh pasta; if using dried pasta, follow the directions on the package. Cook just until tender.
4. Strain the pasta and add to the sauce in the frying pan. Simmer until the sauce clings to the noodles. When almost done, add the peas and then the remaining butter.
5. Transfer to a platter, drizzle with truffle oil, and top with Parmesan and parsley. Serve immediately.

*See "chop," "deglaze," "Parmesan," "reduce," "sauté," "simmer," and "smash" in the Glossary; for blanching, see Tips and Techniques.

Ingredients continued

For the sauce and pappardelle:

3 tablespoons unsalted butter

1 tablespoon chopped garlic

5 cups braised duck mixture

1 cup marinara sauce (see Spaghetti and Meatballs, p. 168)

Salt

2 pounds pappardelle (or fettucine if you can't find pappardelle)

1 cup fresh English peas, blanched*

1/2 ounce white truffle oil

1/2 cup shaved Parmesan*

3 tablespoons chopped parsley

ORECCHIETTE WITH CHICKEN AND GORGONZOLA CREAM SAUCE

Serves 4 to 6

This pasta dish — with its little bits of bacon, the slightly bitter flavor of radicchio, chicken, spinach, creamy Gorgonzola sauce, and walnuts — is one of my favorites. The orecchiette (the word means "little ears" in Italian) work so well because the shape picks up and holds the sauce perfectly. It's easy to make. You can cook the chicken and pasta in advance, so when you're ready to serve, all you need to do is make the sauce.

What You Need

12-inch frying pan   5-quart stockpot

How to Make

1. In the frying pan, add olive oil and cook bacon over medium heat until browned, about 3 minutes.
2. Drain most of the grease and add the garlic to the bacon. Cook for 30 seconds (do not let garlic brown); then add wine and cream.
3. Let sauce reduce* for 3 minutes; then add cheeses, basil, and chicken.
4. Reduce for another 4 minutes; then add cooked pasta and continue reducing until pasta softens and sauce adheres to it.
5. Add walnuts, radicchio, and spinach and toss with the hot pasta just until the greens begin to wilt.
6. Season with salt and pepper to taste, toss in the parsley, and serve.

*See "chop," "Grana Padano," "Parmesan," and "reduce" in the Glossary; for toasting, see Tips and Techniques.

Ingredients

3 tablespoons olive oil
1/2 cup chopped* uncooked bacon
2 tablespoons chopped garlic
1-1/2 cups white wine (of a quality you'd like to drink)
1-1/2 cups heavy cream
3/4 cup crumbled Gorgonzola cheese
1/2 cup grated Parmesan* or Grana Padano*
4 fresh basil leaves
3 6-ounce cooked chicken breasts (they should still be juicy), cut into 1-inch chunks
1 pound orecchiette, cooked al dente (follow direction on the box)
1/2 cup toasted* walnuts
1-1/2 cups chopped radicchio
2 large handfuls baby spinach
Salt and pepper
1/4 cup chopped parsley

BURGUNDY BRAISED BEEF

Serves 4 to 6

I love braising meat. During the hours of cooking, the meat seems to release its essence into the braising liquid and then reabsorbs all that flavor and becomes succulent and even more full-bodied. The chuck in this recipe has enough fat to stay juicy through lengthy cooking. Serve this dish with roasted garlic mashed potatoes or horseradish mashed potatoes (see Mashed Potatoes, p. 191).

What You Need

5- to 6-quart ovenproof roasting pot, such as Le Creuset   Slotted spoon

How to Make

Preheat oven to 500F.

1. Season meat well with salt and pepper and let stand for about 30 minutes.
2. In the pot, heat the olive oil over medium heat until it just begins to smoke.
3. Roll the chuck steaks in the flour until they're well coated; then place them in the roasting pot and brown the meat, about 4 minutes on each side.
4. Drain the excess oil and then add the wine, veal stock, bay leaves, thyme, celery, carrots, parsnips, shallots, garlic, cinnamon stick, mushrooms, tomatoes, tomato paste, and bacon.
5. Cover the pot and place in the oven for 15 minutes; then turn heat down to 375F and let braise for 3-1/2 hours.
6. Pull out pot and let meat rest in the pot for 30 minutes.
7. Carefully remove the meat to a cutting board. With the slotted spoon, take out the vegetables and place on a platter.
8. Slice the meat and arrange on top of the vegetables.
9. Remove the cinnamon stick and bay leaves. The sauce should be almost as thick as gravy. If it's not thick enough, place the roasting pan on the stove and reduce* sauce over medium-high heat until it reaches the desired consistency. If it's too thick, add a little water.
10. When sauce has the right consistency, season with salt and pepper. Add peas and heat for about 30 seconds. Pour sauce over the meat.
11. Garnish with Fried Onions and parsley. Serve family-style.

*See "chop," "reduce," and "smash" in the Glossary.

Ingredients

5 8- to 10-ounce chuck flats
Salt and pepper to taste
1/4 cup olive oil
2 cups all-purpose flour
3 cups good Burgundy wine
6 cups veal stock (see Basic Demi-glace, p. 228) or store-bought beef stock
2 bay leaves
2 sprigs fresh thyme
3 stalks celery, cut into 1-inch pieces
3 carrots, peeled and cut into 1-inch pieces
2 parsnips, peeled and cut into 1-inch pieces
5 shallots, peeled and halved
6 garlic cloves, peeled and smashed*
1 cinnamon stick
14 medium-size mushrooms, cleaned and left whole
1 cup chopped* canned whole tomatoes
2 tablespoons tomato paste
2 pieces bacon, chopped and partially cooked
1/2 cup frozen peas
2 cups Fried Onions (recipe, p. 226)
1/4 cup chopped parsley

BUCATINI AND CLAMS

Serves 4 to 6

Here's a fun and different way to enjoy a clam pasta — use bucatini. Bucatini is a thick spaghetti-like pasta with a hole through the center of each strand, and I really like the way the sauce gets absorbed into the middle of the noodle. It offers a little more bite as well. The sweet clams balance the bucatini's chewy goodness, while the caramelized fennel and onions, tomato, and pancetta provide plenty of robust flavor. (If you can't find bucatini, spaghetti or linguine make a good substitute.)

What You Need

Pasta pot   Large frying pan with lid

How to Make

1. In the pasta pot, bring water to a boil. Add a little olive oil and salt and then the bucatini. Cook according to directions on the package until noodles are tender but still chewy. Save 1/2 cup of pasta water; then drain pasta and set aside.
2. In the frying pan, cook pancetta over low-medium heat. When it is just beginning to brown, add 2 tablespoons of butter, onions, fennel, garlic, and bay leaf and cook slowly until caramelized.*
3. Add tomatoes and cook for 1 minute, just until they start to release their juices. Then add the wine, clam juice, chile flakes, marinara sauce, basil leaves, and clams.
4. Continue to simmer* at low-medium, covered, to steam open the clams, about 2 to 3 minutes.
5. Turn off heat and add the cooked, drained pasta to the pan. The clams should be just barely starting to open.
6. Toss the pasta with the sauce, cover the pan again, and let sit until the clams are completely open. Discard any clams that haven't opened.
7. Add 1 tablespoon butter, olive oil, Grana Padano, chopped parsley, salt, and pepper. If the mixture looks too dry, moisten with a little pasta water.
8. Serve pasta on a platter and place the clams on top. Garnish with basil, fennel, or parsley sprigs.

*See "caramelize," "chop," "dice," "Grana Padano," and "simmer" in the Glossary; for cleaning clams, see Tips and Techniques.

Ingredients

1-1/2 pounds bucatini

3 tablespoons extra-virgin olive oil plus a little for the pasta pot

Salt and pepper to taste

1/2 cup chopped* pancetta or bacon

3 tablespoons unsalted butter

1/2 cup finely diced* red onion

1 cup finely diced fennel

6 garlic cloves, peeled and thinly sliced

1 bay leaf

1 cup diced fresh tomatoes

1/2 cup white wine (of a quality you'd like to drink)

1 cup clam juice

1/4 teaspoon chile flakes

1 cup marinara sauce (see Spaghetti and Meatballs, p. 168)

6 basil leaves

24 to 30 Manila clams, cleaned*

1/2 cup Grana Padano*

1/4 cup chopped Italian parsley

Basil, fennel, or parsley sprigs

HERB-CRUSTED RACK OF LAMB WITH WHOLE-GRAIN MUSTARD DEMI-GLACE

Serves 4

If you love lamb as much as I do, preparing this dish is well worth the time. I serve this classic French-inspired roast with Potato-Spinach Gratin and crispy Fried Onions. It's a wonderful dish for any special occasion.

What You Need

Sauté pan   9 x 13-inch roasting pan   Meat thermometer   2-quart saucepan
Mixing bowl   Whisk

How to Make

Preheat oven to 375F.

1. Season lamb with salt and pepper.
2. In the sauté pan, add olive oil over medium-high heat. When oil is hot, add the lamb and sear the racks on both sides, about 3 minutes per side. Let cool.
3. Brush each lamb rack with Dijon mustard.
4. Mix the bread crumbs with the rosemary, thyme, tarragon, parsley, and garlic. Pack the mixture onto each piece of lamb, leaving the bones alone.
5. Cover the bones with pieces of foil. Bake the lamb for about 20 to 25 minutes, or until the racks register an internal temperature of about 118F on a meat thermometer. Heat the Potato-Spinach Gratin, covered, while you're cooking the lamb.
6. When lamb is done, remove from oven and let racks rest for at least 10 minutes. Place a piece of Potato-Spinach Gratin on each of four plates.
7. In the saucepan, heat the Basic Demi-glace. When it's warm, whisk in whole-grain mustard and butter. Season with salt and pepper to taste.
8. Cut each 4-bone rack in half. Put one half against the piece of Potato-Spinach Gratin; then cut the other half into two chops and fan them out on each plate. Drizzle the Basic Demi-glace around each plate, top with Fried Onions, and serve.

*See "chop" in the Glossary.

Ingredients

2 racks of lamb (about 8 bones each), cut in half
Salt and pepper to taste
3 tablespoons olive oil
2 tablespoons Dijon mustard
1-1/2 cups plain bread crumbs
2 tablespoons chopped* fresh rosemary
2 tablespoons chopped fresh thyme
2 tablespoons chopped fresh tarragon
2 tablespoons chopped Italian parsley
1 tablespoon chopped garlic
1 cup Basic Demi-glace (recipe, p. 228)
1 tablespoon whole-grain mustard
2 tablespoons unsalted butter
4 pieces Potato-Spinach Gratin (recipe, p. 196)
1 cup Fried Onions (recipe, p. 226)

PAN-ROASTED SEA BASS WITH ARTICHOKE RISOTTO AND HEIRLOOM TOMATO VINAIGRETTE

Serves 4

Fresh bluenose sea bass or white sea bass are the right choices for this dish. The bass's semi-firm, flaky flesh makes it a fine accompaniment for the risotto and braised baby artichokes. The tangy heirloom tomato vinaigrette that finishes the presentation adds zest as well as color. Make this at the beginning of fall when heirloom tomatoes are still abundant and sea bass is at its best.

This recipe requires some multitasking so that you can bring everything to the table at the same time. Just be sure to keep an eye on the fish and make sure it doesn't get overcooked while you're making the risotto.

What You Need

Whisk   Large bowl   12-inch frying pan   12-inch ovenproof frying pan, such as cast iron   Wooden spoon   Mixing bowl   4-quart saucepan or stockpot

How to Make

FOR THE ARTICHOKES:

1. For each artichoke, cut about a quarter off the top and trim the tough skin off the stem. Remove the outer leaves until the light yellow leaves are exposed. Cut in half and remove the red leaves in the center. Place artichoke halves in enough cold water to cover, add 1/4 cup lemon juice, and soak until ready to cook.
2. Heat the frying pan and add 3 tablespoons of olive oil.
3. Dry the artichokes on a towel. Combine in a bowl with the anchovies, garlic, and a pinch of chile flakes.
4. Brown the seasoned artichokes over medium heat for about 5 minutes. Add chicken stock, wine, and thyme.
5. Cover and braise over medium-high heat for about 15 minutes. Check to see if the artichokes are beginning to feel soft. Continue cooking until the liquid has reduced* and forms a glaze on the artichokes.
6. Pull off the heat. Squeeze on the lemon juice and add 2 tablespoons olive oil, salt and pepper to taste, and parsley.

Ingredients

For the artichokes:
20 baby artichokes
1/4 cup lemon juice plus juice of 2 lemons
5 tablespoons olive oil
3 anchovies, chopped* into a paste
1 tablespoon chopped garlic
Chile flakes
1-1/2 cups Homemade Chicken Stock (recipe, p. 234) or store-bought low-sodium
1 cup white wine (of a quality you'd like to drink)
1 tablespoon chopped fresh thyme
Salt and pepper
3 tablespoons chopped parsley

FOR THE HEIRLOOM TOMATO VINAIGRETTE:

Whisk all ingredients together and add salt and pepper to taste. The vinaigrette should resemble a loose salsa. Let sit for at least 15 minutes.

FOR THE ARTICHOKE RISOTTO AND SEA BASS:

Preheat oven to 400F.

1. In the saucepan, heat chicken stock over medium heat until it's at a high simmer,* about 5 to 10 minutes. While stock is warming up, heat the oven-proof frying pan over medium-high heat.
2. Salt and pepper the fish fillets. When the pan is hot, add 5 tablespoons of olive oil and then the fish immediately. (Note: When sautéing fish, heat the pan first and then add cold oil. This creates an air pocket that helps keep the fish from sticking.)
3. Sauté* fish on one side for 1 minute on top of the stove; then put the pan in the oven. Bake for about 6 minutes, depending on the thickness of the fillets.
4. While fish is baking, in a separate pan, heat 4 tablespoons olive oil over medium heat and sauté onions until they are slightly translucent, about 4 minutes.
5. Add the rice to the onions and sauté for 2 minutes; then add bay leaf and artichokes. Add the lemon zest and basil leaves and, with a wooden spoon, stir in about half the hot stock. Keep stirring the risotto and adding stock as it cooks in.
6. Check the fish, and when the tops of the fillets have turned a crisp golden brown, turn them over and cook the other side for 2 more minutes, basting with the oil. When the fish feels semi-firm, it's done. Pull out of the oven and let rest for 5 minutes.
7. Meanwhile, keep adding hot stock and stirring the risotto. The process should take about 15 minutes. The rice is done when the grains look plump and moist. It shouldn't be overcooked. If you aren't sure, taste a rice grain or two to check the consistency. It should be soft but with a little chewiness inside.
8. Add the Parmesan, butter, salt, and pepper. If the risotto is too thick, add a little more stock or water. It should look creamy.
9. Put about 3/4 cup of risotto in the center of each of four plates; then place a fillet on the risotto. Top the fish with the heirloom tomato vinaigrette and spread more vinaigrette on the plate as a garnish. Serve right away.

*See "chop," "dice," "Parmesan," "reduce," "sauté," and "simmer" in the Glossary.

Ingredients continued

For the heirloom tomato vinaigrette (makes 1-1/2 cups):

3/4 cup diced* heirloom tomatoes
1/2 cup halved yellow and red grape tomatoes
1 teaspoon chopped garlic
1 tablespoon chopped shallots
2 tablespoons chopped fresh basil
2 tablespoons chopped parsley
1/4 cup finely chopped red onion
3 tablespoons sherry vinegar
4 tablespoons extra-virgin olive oil
1 tablespoon lemon juice
Salt and pepper

For the artichoke risotto and sea bass:

5 cups Homemade Chicken Stock (recipe, p. 234) or store-bought low-sodium
4 6-ounce sea bass fillets
Salt and pepper to taste
9 tablespoons olive oil
1/2 cup finely diced onions
1 cup Arborio rice
1 bay leaf
1-1/2 cups braised baby artichokes, quartered
1 tablespoon lemon zest
3 basil leaves
1/2 cup grated Parmesan*
3 tablespoons butter
1 cup heirloom tomato vinaigrette

ALASKAN HALIBUT WITH CLAM SAUCE

Serves 4

The clean flavor and flaky texture of fresh halibut make it a reliable choice for cooking. Almost any sauce goes well with it. This dish pairs halibut fillets with my version of clam beurre blanc, a butter sauce based on fresh clams, tomatoes, and thyme.

What You Need

12-inch frying pan with lid

How to Make

1. Season the halibut with salt and pepper. Dip the presentation side of each fillet in the flour.
2. Heat the frying pan and add olive and canola oils.
3. Put fish in the pan flour side down. Cook over medium-high heat until lightly browned, about 3 to 4 minutes.
4. Flip fish and drain excess oil from the pan. Leave fish in the pan.
5. Add clams, shallots, tomatoes, wine, cream, lemon juice, basil, and thyme. Cover and cook over medium-high heat for about 5 minutes.
6. When the clams have opened and the fish feels firm, remove both from the pan, leaving the vegetables and liquid. Discard clams that haven't opened.
7. Put 1/2 cup of orzo on each of four plates and then place a piece of fish on top. Scatter the clams around and on top of the fish.
8. Reduce* the sauce over medium-high heat until it starts to thicken, about 3 minutes.
9. Pull off the heat and whip in the butter. Taste and adjust for salt, pepper, and lemon.
10. Pour the sauce on and around the fish. Serve hot.

*See "chop," "dice," and "reduce" in the Glossary; for cleaning clams, see Tips and Techniques.

Ingredients

4 6-ounce halibut fillets (or any flaky white fish)
Salt and pepper to taste
1/3 cup flour
2 tablespoons olive oil
3 tablespoons canola oil
20 Manila clams, cleaned*
3 tablespoons finely chopped* shallots
1 cup peeled, seeded, and diced* tomatoes
1-1/3 cups white wine (of a quality you'd like to drink)
1/2 cup heavy cream
1 tablespoon lemon juice
2 fresh basil leaves
2 sprigs fresh thyme
2 cups cooked orzo or rice
4 tablespoons unsalted butter

GRILLED SALMON WITH SUCCOTASH

Serves 4

Toast customers clamor for this dish in the summer, when corn is at its sweetest.

The salmon is garnished with red pepper vinaigrette and teamed with succotash, a combination that really shows off the flavors of each ingredient. A garnish of watercress, simply dressed with olive oil and lemon, plus a scatter of Fried Leeks or Fried Onions complete the presentation.

What You Need

Blender   Mixing bowl   12-inch frying pan   Grill

How to Make

FOR THE RED PEPPER VINAIGRETTE:

1. In the blender, add everything except the olive and canola oils. Turn speed to high and slowly add both oils. Process just until the mixture is emulsified and smooth.
2. Pour into the bowl and add salt and pepper to taste. Set aside.

Ingredients

For the red pepper vinaigrette (makes about 3/4 cup):

1/2 cup roasted red peppers,* seeded and peeled

1 teaspoon honey

1/2 teaspoon diced* chipotle chile or half of any small red chile

1/4 teaspoon chopped* garlic

2 tablespoons lemon juice

1 tablespoon champagne vinegar

3 teaspoons olive oil

2 tablespoons canola oil

Salt and pepper

FOR THE SUCCOTASH AND SALMON:

1. Heat the frying pan over medium-high heat. Add 2 tablespoons of butter and heat until it melts and begins to lightly brown.
2. Add the onions, garlic, a pinch of chili powder, and a pinch of cumin. Sauté* for 2 minutes and then add the corn, bell peppers, and zucchinis. Cook until vegetables start to caramelize,* about 4 to 5 more minutes.
3. Deglaze* the pan with wine and cook until the wine evaporates, another 2 minutes.
4. Add 1 tablespoon butter along with salt and pepper to taste. Keep warm.
5. Heat the grill to medium high. Rub salmon with 2 tablespoons of olive oil and season with salt and pepper. Grill* until the outside starts to crisp, about 4-1/2 minutes on each side. The interior should be flaky and a little translucent.
6. Place equal amounts of hot succotash in the center of each of four plates and then set a piece of salmon alongside. Drizzle the red pepper vinaigrette around the edges of the succotash.
7. Toss the watercress with 2 tablespoons olive oil, salt, pepper, and lemon juice and divide equally among the plates. Finish with a scatter of Fried Onions or Fried Leeks.

*See "caramelize," "chop," "deglaze," "dice," and "sauté" in the Glossary; for grilling and roasting peppers, see Tips and Techniques.

Ingredients continued

For the succotash and salmon:
(Note: All the vegetables should be chopped to the same size as the corn kernels.)
3 tablespoons unsalted butter
1/2 cup diced red onion
1 teaspoon chopped garlic
Chili powder
Ground cumin
4 cups sweet white corn kernels, fresh or frozen
1/4 cup finely diced red pepper
1/4 cup finely diced green bell pepper
1 cup finely diced green zucchini
1 cup finely diced yellow zucchini
1/4 cup white wine (of a quality you'd like to drink)
Salt and pepper to taste
4 7-ounce fillets of salmon, bones removed
4 tablespoons olive oil
3/4 cup red pepper vinaigrette
1 bunch watercress
Juice of 1 lemon
1 cup Fried Leeks (recipe, p. 200) or Fried Onions (recipe, p. 226)

GARLIC-ROASTED DUNGENESS CRAB

Serves 4 to 6

This wonderful dish celebrates the sweet flavor of Dungeness crab. It makes a great meal served with a little spaghettini tossed with basil, garlic, and olive oil; a simple green salad; and hot sourdough bread for dipping in the sauce. Wash it down with a chilled Chardonnay. It's fun to eat the crab with your hands and a pleasure to share the dish, and the experience, with friends and family.

What You Need

9 x 13-inch roasting pan

How to Make

Preheat oven to 450F.

1. Heat the roasting pan on the stove at medium-high heat and add olive oil and garlic. Cook until garlic just starts to turn light brown, about 1 minute.
2. Add chile flakes, shallots, bay leaf, and crab pieces.
3. Toss the crab in the flavored oil.
4. Squeeze in the juice of 2 lemons and then add the lemon halves to the pan. Add wine and half the butter along with salt and pepper to taste.
5. Toss a couple more times to make sure the ingredients are mixed; then put in the oven and bake, uncovered, for about 15 minutes.
6. Pull out of the oven and add the rest of the butter and the parsley. Toss again, making sure all the crab pieces are coated and steaming hot.
7. Serve immediately right out of the pan.

*See "chop" in the Glossary.

Ingredients

1/4 cup extra-virgin olive oil
15 garlic cloves, peeled and
   sliced thin
1/4 teaspoon chile flakes
4 tablespoons chopped*
   shallots
1 bay leaf
At least 3 cooked Dungeness
   crabs (about 1-1/2 pounds
   each), cleaned and cracked
   into pieces but with shells on
3 lemons, halved
1 cup white wine (of a quality
   you'd like to drink)
1/2 cup melted unsalted butter
Salt and pepper
1/3 cup chopped Italian parsley

PARMESAN-CRUSTED PETRALE SOLE WITH ARTICHOKE BEURRE BLANC AND PECAN RICE PILAF

Serves 4

This is a favorite at our Mill Valley restaurant. The artichoke butter sauce is a perfect complement to the mild-flavored petrale sole. Other types of sole or white fish will also work with this recipe. I use veal stock in the pecan rice pilaf for a richer flavor.

What You Need

2-quart saucepan   3-quart stockpot   Mixing bowl1   12-inch frying pan   Whisk

How to Make

FOR THE PECAN RICE PILAF:

1. In the stockpot, melt 1 tablespoon of butter over medium heat and sauté* onions, pecans, and bay leaf for about 4 minutes.
2. Add rice. (Note: If using regular white or brown rice, cooking time will be longer.) Stir everything well and add veal stock.
3. Bring to a boil over medium-high heat; then cover, turn down heat, and cook at a low simmer* for 15 minutes until all liquid is absorbed. Remove bay leaf.
4. Add 1 tablespoon butter, salt, and pepper. Cover and set aside.

FOR THE ARTICHOKE BEURRE BLANC:

1. In the saucepan over medium-high heat, reduce* the wine, clam juice, cream, shallots, and artichokes until the mixture starts to have a molten look, about 15 minutes.
2. Pull off the heat and whip in the butter with the whisk; then add the lemon juice, salt, and pepper. Set aside to rest, making sure to pick a place that's not too hot; excess heat will cause the butterfat to separate, "breaking" the sauce.
3. If the sauce looks too thick, add a few drops of hot water and whisk in.

Ingredients

For the pecan rice pilaf:

2 tablespoons unsalted butter
1/3 cup finely diced* yellow onion
1/3 cup chopped* pecans
1 bay leaf
1 cup converted white rice
1-1/2 cups veal stock (see Basic Demi-glace, p. 228)
Salt and pepper to taste

For the artichoke beurre blanc (makes about 2 cups):

1 cup white wine, such as Chardonnay (of a quality you'd like to drink)
1/2 cup clam juice
1/2 cup cream
2 tablespoons chopped shallots
1 cup braised baby artichokes* (if using canned, choose artichoke hearts packed in water, not oil)
5 tablespoons unsalted butter
Juice of half a lemon
Salt and pepper to taste

FOR THE PETRALE SOLE:

1. Season sole fillets with salt and pepper.
2. Mix together the panko bread crumbs and Parmesan.
3. In the bowl, whisk eggs with a little water.
4. Dip each fillet in the whisked eggs and then in the panko-Parmesan mixture.
5. Heat the frying pan over medium heat and add both oils; then add the fillets, in batches if necessary so you won't crowd the fillets. Brown them on one side, about 4 minutes; then flip and brown the other side, about 4 minutes more.
6. Between batches, be sure to remove crumbs and brown bits from the pan. Add more oil if necessary.
7. When all the fillets are done, spoon about 1/2 cup of rice pilaf into the center of each of four plates. Place 2 pieces of fish on top of the pilaf and cover with artichoke beurre blanc. Serve immediately.

*See "chop," "dice," "Parmesan," "reduce," "sauté," and "simmer" in the Glossary; for artichokes, see Tips and Techniques.

Ingredients continued

For the petrale sole:

8 3-ounce sole fillets
Salt and pepper to taste
1-1/2 cups panko bread crumbs
3/4 cup grated Parmesan*
5 eggs
3 tablespoons olive oil
1/4 cup canola oil
2 cups pecan rice pilaf
1-1/2 cups artichoke beurre blanc

CLASSICS

CLASSICS

These are the dishes that take you back to childhood. They are relatively easy to make yet always satisfying for the whole family. We're not reinventing the wheel here, just making good, wholesome food. Remember when your mom would dish up a platter of spaghetti and meatballs? Remember the excitement you felt when you saw the steam rising out of a freshly baked chicken pot pie? I hope the recipes in this chapter will revive your memories of your favorite childhood foods.

SPAGHETTI AND MEATBALLS

Serves 6 to 8

This classic dish is served in many homes and is a staple in thousands of restaurants because it's a favorite comfort food for children and adults alike. Cooking the pasta and preparing the meatballs are both pretty fast. Making a great marinara takes some time, but it's worth it.

What You Need

Food processor   5-quart stockpot   Large storage container   Mixing bowl
Cookie sheet   12-inch sauté pan

How to Make

FOR THE MARINARA SAUCE:

1. In the food processor, add garlic, carrots, celery, and onions and chop fine.
2. In the stockpot over medium-high heat, combine the puréed and crushed tomatoes with chopped garlic, carrots, celery, and onions.
3. Add water plus oregano, dried and fresh basil, sugar, bay leaf, olive oil, and salt. Bring to a boil.
4. Turn heat to medium-low and simmer,* stirring from the bottom, for about 3 hours. Sauce is done when it's thick enough to coat a spoon.
5. Transfer to the container to cool. Refrigerate overnight to let the flavors bind.

Ingredients

For the marinara sauce:

10 garlic cloves, peeled and
    chopped*
2 cups carrots chunks
3 celery stalks, chopped
1 medium yellow onion, chopped
4 28-ounce cans whole peeled
    Roma tomatoes, puréed
1 28-ounce can crushed
    tomatoes
4 cups water
2 tablespoons dried oregano
2 tablespoons dried basil
1/2 cup finely chopped fresh
    basil
1 tablespoon granulated sugar
1 bay leaf
1/4 cup olive oil
1 tablespoon salt

FOR THE SPAGHETTI AND MEATBALLS:

Preheat oven to 350F.

1. Soak bread in milk until the milk is well absorbed.
2. Combine soaked bread with beef, sausage, Parmesan, oregano, basil, parsley, egg, garlic, celery, onion, Worcestershire sauce, salt, and pepper. Mix well. The mixture should feel soft, not too tight.
3. Shape 3-ounce balls, about 2 inches in diameter, and place on the cookie sheet. You should have about 15 meatballs.
4. Bake for 15 to 18 minutes or until meatballs are browned and feel a little bouncy.
5. Pull meatballs out of oven and transfer some to the sauté pan. They won't all fit, so you'll have to cook them in batches. Add marinara sauce, enough to cover, and simmer over medium-low heat until meatballs absorb some sauce, about 5 minutes. Repeat with the next batch of meatballs, adding marinara sauce as needed, until all are done.
6. While meatballs are simmering, fill the stockpot with water and bring to a boil. Add salt and then cook spaghetti according to the directions on the box.
7. Drain the pasta and toss with a little olive oil and salt.
8. Place spaghetti on a large platter; then spoon hot meatballs and sauce on top. Garnish with Parmesan and parsley and serve immediately.

*See "chop," "Parmesan," and "simmer" in the Glossary.

Ingredients continued

For the spaghetti and meatballs:

1-1/2 cups diced sourdough bread, crusts removed

1 cup milk

2 pounds ground beef

6 ounces bulk Italian sausage meat

1/2 cup grated Parmesan* plus more for garnish

1 tablespoon dried oregano

1/4 cup chopped fresh basil

1/4 cup chopped Italian parsley

1 egg, whisked

1 tablespoon chopped garlic

1/4 cup finely chopped celery

1/3 cup finely chopped onion

2 tablespoons Worcestershire sauce

Salt and pepper to taste

3 pounds spaghetti

6 cups marinara sauce

Olive oil

1/4 cup chopped parsley

BUTTERMILK FRIED CHICKEN

Serves 4

At Toast, we've put a lot of time and effort into perfecting this recipe. Now, twenty pounds later (my scale even laughs at me), I think I've got it exactly the way I like it. It does take a little time to prepare properly, but good things do take time. Skillet frying would be the best way to cook the chicken, although this recipe also works in a deep-fryer. (A safety reminder: When frying food, be sure there are no children in the kitchen. The oil is very hot and can cause serious injury.)

What You Need

Large storage container with lid   Mixing bowl   Sheet pan   Rack
Large deep-sided cast iron frying pan with tight-fitting lid or 8-quart deep-fryer
Candy thermometer   Meat thermometer   Whisk

How to Make

1. Wash and dry the chicken.
2. In the storage container, mix together buttermilk, garlic, thyme sprigs, and bay leaf. Add chicken pieces, cover, and marinate in the refrigerator at least 6 hours, preferably overnight.
3. In the bowl, mix flour, garlic and onion powders, baking soda, 1 tablespoon salt, 1 teaspoon pepper, 1 tablespoon sage, cayenne, and 1 tablespoon thyme. Set aside.
4. Lay chicken out on the sheet pan and season with salt and pepper.
5. Dip chicken pieces in the seasoned flour, making sure they're well coated, packing it on. Set chicken pieces on the rack and refrigerate, uncovered, for about 1 hour.
6. Heat Crisco in the frying pan. If you don't have a large enough pan, fry* the chicken in small batches, to avoid crowding. With the candy thermometer, check the oil temperature; it should be about 300F. Lay the chicken pieces in the frying pan and cover with the lid. Be sure to keep the oil temperature at about 300F. If it is too hot, the pieces will burn before they are cooked.
7. Turn the chicken pieces when they're golden brown on one side and cook evenly on the other side, about 8 to 10 minutes per side. Put the lid back on the pan after turning the pieces so the chicken will steam evenly. The whole process should take about 20 minutes per batch.
8. When the chicken is almost done, remove lid and continue to cook so that the pieces become browned and crisp. With a meat thermometer, check the center of the big pieces to make sure they are at 160F.
9. Remove chicken and let cool on a rack lined with paper towels for a few minutes.
10. Drain cooking oil from the frying pan into a can, but keep the crusty bits left from frying the chicken. Add butter and flour to the pan and stir together over medium heat, incorporating well.
11. Add chicken stock and cream. Reduce* over medium-high heat for 3 to 5 minutes while stirring well with a whisk. Add 1/2 teaspoon sage and 1/2 teaspoon thyme. By now, the gravy should be about the consistency of heavy cream. If it's too thick, thin with a little more stock. Salt and pepper to taste.
12. Place chicken pieces on plates and serve with gravy, Mashed Potatoes (recipe, p. 191), corn on the cob, and Buttermilk Biscuits (recipe, p. 182).

*See "reduce" and "smash" in the Glossary; for frying, see Tips and Techniques.

Ingredients

2 cups buttermilk

3 garlic cloves, peeled and smashed*

6 thyme sprigs

1 bay leaf

1 3-pound frying chicken, cut into wings, drumettes, thighs, legs, and halved breasts, backbone removed and a couple of holes poked in thighs (ask the butcher to do this for you)

3 cups flour

3 tablespoons garlic powder

3 tablespoons onion powder

1 teaspoon baking soda

1 tablespoon salt plus more to taste

1 teaspoon black pepper plus more to taste

1 tablespoon plus 1/2 teaspoon ground sage

1/2 teaspoon cayenne pepper

1 tablespoon plus 1/2 teaspoon dried thyme

2 cups Crisco, canola oil, or peanut oil

2 tablespoons unsalted butter

4 tablespoons flour

2 cups Homemade Chicken Stock (recipe, p. 234) or store-bought low-sodium

1/4 cup cream

CLASSIC MEATLOAF

Serves 4

Of all American comfort foods, this is one of the most basic. Everyone seems to have a meatloaf recipe, but some versions are much more satisfying than others. Mine is straight-forward, with simple flavors enriched by a creamy mushroom gravy. I think it's a classic. Serve with Mashed Potatoes (recipe, p. 191) and peas and carrots. What could be more comforting?

What You Need

Mixing bowl   14 x 10-1/2-inch roasting pan   Meat thermometer   Spatula
Clear heat-proof bowl   2-quart saucepan

How to Make

Preheat oven to 375F.

1. In a bowl, mix together ground beef, bread, eggs, ketchup, Parmesan, bell pepper, onion, 1 tablespoon basil, thyme, tarragon, and Worcestershire and Tabasco sauces. Knead gently until all ingredients are combined.
2. Form into a firm loaf and place in the middle of the roasting pan. Smooth a little ketchup on top with the back of a spoon and season with salt and pepper.
3. Add 1 cup of water to the roasting pan.
4. Bake for about 1 hour or until the internal temperature reaches 140F on the meat thermometer.
5. Pull meatloaf out of the oven and let rest for 15 minutes. Carefully remove from pan with the spatula and place on a serving dish.
6. Pour the roasting liquid in the pan into the clear heat-proof bowl.
7. In the saucepan, melt butter and sauté* mushrooms, 1/2 teaspoon basil, and shallots over medium heat until softened, about 3 minutes.
8. Add the flour. Mix well, making sure all the flour is blended in with the vegetables.
9. Add the roasting liquid, cream, chicken stock, and bay leaf; then stir well until the gravy begins to thicken, about 4 minutes. Season with salt and pepper. If the gravy becomes too thick, add a little milk.
10. Slice meatloaf, transfer slices to plates, and pour some mushroom gravy over each slice.

*See "dice," "Parmesan," and "sauté" in the Glossary.

Ingredients

2-1/2 pounds ground beef (preferably 20 percent fat)
1/2 cup diced sourdough bread, crusts removed
2 eggs
1/3 cup ketchup plus more for topping
1/4 cup grated Parmesan*
1 green bell pepper, finely diced*
1 cup finely diced yellow onion
1 tablespoon plus 1/2 teaspoon dried basil
1 teaspoon dried thyme
1 tablespoon dried tarragon
2 tablespoons Worcestershire sauce
2 tablespoons Tabasco sauce
Salt and pepper to taste
1 cup water
3 tablespoons unsalted butter
3/4 cup sliced crimini mushrooms
2 tablespoons finely diced shallots
3 tablespoons flour
1 cup of the roasting liquid, fat skimmed off
1/2 cup cream
1 bay leaf
Milk
1-1/4 cups Homemade Chicken Stock (recipe, p. 234) or store-bought low-sodium

SHRIMP SCAMPI

Serves 4 to 6

"Shrimp scampi" actually translates as "shrimp shrimp," because "scampi" is Italian for "shrimp." An Italian American classic, the word "scampi" on American menus became synonymous with a buttery garlic sauce.

   I love the fact that this dish is so easy to prepare. The only thing that takes a little time is the butter sauce, and you can make that a couple of hours before you serve the shrimp. Then just heat up your broiler, and in 5 minutes, you'll have beautifully caramelized garlicky scampi. Serve with pecan rice pilaf (see Parmesan-Crusted Petrale Sole with Artichoke Beurre Blanc and Pecan Rice Pilaf, p. 162), steamed asparagus, and sourdough bread for dipping in the sauce.

What You Need

12-inch frying pan   9 x 13-inch glass baking dish   2-quart saucepan   Whisk

How to Make

1. Salt and pepper the shrimp. Sear in the frying pan over medium-high heat until rare, about 1 minute per side.
2. Remove shrimp from pan and put them in the baking dish.
3. In the saucepan over medium-high heat, add the wine, cream, clam juice, shallots, and bay leaf and reduce* until the mixture is bubbling and thickened, about 20 minutes.
4. Pull off the heat, remove bay leaf, and whip in butter, garlic, and the juice of 1 lemon along with salt and pepper.
5. Pour sauce over the shrimp in the baking dish. Squeeze 1 lemon over the shrimp and sprinkle with paprika. Cut 2 lemons into wedges.
6. Broil shrimp for 3 to 4 minutes or until browned and caramelized. Sprinkle with parsley and serve with a couple of lemon wedges.

*See "chop" and "reduce" in the Glossary; for deveining, see Tips and Techniques.

Ingredients

40 large (16/20 count) shrimp, peeled and deveined,* with tails on

Salt and pepper to taste

1-1/2 cups buttery Chardonnay (of a quality you'd like to drink)

1 cup cream

1 cup clam juice

3 shallots, chopped*

1 bay leaf

1 cup (2 sticks) unsalted butter

1/3 cup chopped garlic

4 lemons

1 tablespoon paprika

1/4 cup chopped parsley

FISH AND CHIPS

Serves 4 to 6

Halibut is perfect for this dish because its firm yet tender texture and sweet, distinct flavor stand out against the light, crispy coating. If halibut is not available, cod is the next best choice, and any white fish that is not too firm also works well. A batch of Crispy French Fries completes this classic combination. Serve with the traditional malt vinegar, tartar sauce, and Jicama-Apple Coleslaw (recipe, p. 186).

What You Need

Deep-fryer or 12-inch deep-sided frying pan and cooking thermometer
Mixing bowl   Rack

How to Make

FOR THE BEER BATTER:

In the bowl, combine all ingredients and mix well to form a light-textured batter. Set aside.

FOR THE FISH:

1. In the deep-fryer, heat Crisco to 350F. The oil should be at least 1 inch deep.
2. Season the fish strips with salt and pepper; then dredge* in flour, letting strips sit in the flour for a couple of minutes.
3. When oil is ready, dip the floured fish in the beer batter, making sure the strips are completely coated. Shake off any excess batter.
4. Gently lay battered fish in the hot oil. Do not crowd. Shake the deep-fryer basket once to make sure pieces of fish are not stuck on the bottom. Try not to move them around too much as they fry;* let the batter cook and adhere to the fish.
5. When the edges of the strips become crisp and brown, about 3 minutes, turn each strip over and cook the other side, about another 3 minutes. Remove to the rack to dry when done.
6. Serve with Crispy French Fries.

*See "dredge" in the Glossary; for frying, see Tips and Techniques.

Ingredients

For the beer batter:

2 cups all-purpose flour
1 bottle Red Tail Ale or other
    amber ale
1-1/4 cups water
1/2 teaspoon baking soda
1/2 teaspoon paprika
1/2 teaspoon garlic powder
1/2 teaspoon onion powder
1 teaspoon salt
1/4 teaspoon black pepper

For the fish:

1-1/2 cups Crisco
12 1- to 1-1/2-ounce pieces of
    halibut, cut into strips
Salt and pepper to taste
1 cup flour
Beer batter
5 to 6 cups Crispy French Fries
    (recipe, p. 198)

CHICKEN POT PIE

Makes 4 16-ounce crocks or 1 2-quart casserole

Homemade chicken pot pie is one of the most sensuous American classics I know. It combines flaky pastry with a luscious stew of chicken, corn, carrots, peas, and potatoes in a rich, thyme-flecked gravy. The filling is easy to make, and the pastry isn't too difficult either. You can save time by using a good-quality frozen pie crust or puff pastry, such as Dufour Pastry Kitchens.

What You Need

5-quart stockpot   Mixing bowl   Hand-held pizza cutter   Rubber spatula
Rolling pin   4 16-ounce crocks or 1 2-quart casserole   Pastry brush

How to Make

FOR THE CHICKEN AND VEGETABLE STEW:

1. In the stockpot, melt the butter and sauté* onions, carrots, celery, and chicken over medium-high heat until chicken is partially cooked, about 5 minutes.
2. Add thyme, basil, and bay leaf and stir.
3. Blend in the flour and cook for about 3 to 4 minutes. If the mixture looks dry, add a little more butter.
4. When all the flour is well incorporated, add chicken stock and stir well. Keep stirring from the bottom of the pot until the stew starts to thicken.
5. Turn the heat down to a simmer* and stir every few minutes. Cook for another 15 minutes.
6. Add the peas, potatoes, and corn. Stir in well. If the stew looks too thick, add a little more stock, but, remember, it's a pie filling and shouldn't be soupy.
7. Add salt and pepper to taste and pull off the heat. Transfer to a shallower dish and let cool. Refrigerate, ideally overnight, before filling and baking the pies.

Ingredients

For the chicken and vegetable stew:

5 tablespoons unsalted butter plus more if needed
1/2 cup yellow onions, diced*
2 carrots, peeled and diced
2 stalks celery, diced
3 cups diced boneless, skinless chicken breast, uncooked
1/2 teaspoon fresh thyme
1/2 teaspoon dried basil
1 bay leaf
1-1/2 cups all-purpose flour
7 to 8 cups Homemade Chicken Stock (recipe, p. 234) or store-bought low-sodium
1/2 cup frozen peas
1 cup boiled, diced red potato
1/2 cup fresh sweet corn kernels (canned or frozen is OK)
Salt and pepper

FOR THE POT PIES:

1. Mix flour and salt.
2. Add butter and shortening and cut into the flour with a pizza cutter or two forks. The mixture should look coarse, with the texture of wet sand.
3. Make a well in the middle of the flour mixture and add egg yolks and water. With a rubber spatula, mix in quickly until it forms a dough. If it looks dry, add a little more water.
4. Working quickly with your hands for a couple of seconds, form the dough into a rough ball. Cover tightly with plastic wrap and refrigerate for 30 minutes.
5. Remove dough from the refrigerator. On a clean work surface, sprinkle a little flour and knead the dough for about 4 to 5 minutes, overlapping and turning it, until it feels elastic and a little bouncy. Then roll it out to about 1/8-inch thickness and cover with a damp towel so it doesn't dry out.
6. Preheat oven to 375F.
7. Fill the crocks with the chilled chicken and vegetable stew.
8. Cut the dough to fit over the top of each crock, leaving a little extra to hang over. Tuck the excess dough around the lip of the dish, making sure it fits tightly. Poke a small hole in the middle of the crust.
9. Beat the egg with 2 tablespoons of water to make an egg wash and brush it over the crusts with the pastry brush.
10. Place the crocks in the oven and bake for about 20 minutes (about 30 to 35 minutes for the casserole). The pot pies are done when the dough is nicely browned and you see a little gravy bubbling in the middle.
11. Let sit for 10 minutes before serving.

*See "dice," "sauté," and "simmer" in the Glossary.

Ingredients continued

For the pot pies:

4 cups all-purpose flour
2 teaspoons salt
2/3 cup cold butter, diced
2/3 cup Crisco
2 egg yolks
1/2 cup cold water plus a little more if needed
Chicken and vegetable stew
1 egg

SIDE DISHES

SIDE DISHES

Serving the right sides with a meal brings everything together. What's fried chicken without hot cornbread or biscuits and mashed potatoes? Isn't a grilled steak enhanced by decadent blue cheese fries, and doesn't poached fish come into its own when accompanied by a beautiful rice pilaf? Components like these work to round out a meal and make for a satisfying as well as more interesting dining experience. Ideal sides will complement and highlight the flavor of your main dish. When composing a plate, always think about what would make the central element shine. What textures and flavors can really bring out its character?

BUTTERMILK BISCUITS

Serves 10 to 12

Almost any breakfast tastes better accompanied by hot biscuits, butter, and honey. Or try them with Meat Gravy for Biscuits and Gravy (recipe, p. 232) for another special treat, the stuff of American breakfast legend.

These biscuits are pretty easy to prepare, and the more practice you get, the better you will be at making them. Remember not to over-knead the dough. Working gently with your hands is the best way to go. Rolling pins overdevelop the gluten, making the biscuits dense instead of light and fluffy.

You can freeze the raw biscuits for up to a month so that there will always be some handy when you want them.

What You Need

Large mixing bowl   Cookie sheet

How to Make

Preheat oven to 450F.

1. In the bowl, mix all the dry ingredients together.
2. Add the cold butter and gently work into the dry ingredients with your hands. Dough should have a lumpy consistency.
3. Add the buttermilk and mix only until ingredients are just combined. If the dough looks too dry, add a little more buttermilk.
4. Turn out dough onto a flat, floured surface. Pat it out gently until it's about 1 inch thick; then fold in half and pat out gently to about 1-inch thickness. Repeat two more times, patting dough out four times altogether.
5. Cut dough into 2-1/2-inch squares with a knife or cut out round biscuits with a cookie cutter.
6. Place biscuits on an ungreased cookie sheet, brush the tops with melted butter, and bake until they are raised and golden brown, about 15 to 18 minutes. Serve hot.

Ingredients

2 cups all-purpose flour plus more for dusting
1/4 teaspoon baking soda
1-1/2 tablespoons baking powder
1 teaspoon kosher salt
6 tablespoons cold unsalted butter, cut into small pieces
3/4 cup buttermilk
3 tablespoons melted butter

CORNBREAD WITH JALAPEÑO AND CHEDDAR

Makes 1 dozen muffins

Really good cornbread jazzed up with a little spice goes well with so many dishes. Serve a hot basket of cornbread with breakfast or dinner. The batter can be made a day in advance and baked when needed. Slather some sweet cream butter on a piping hot piece for a decadent treat.

I like to bake this bread in a muffin tin so each piece is a uniform shape. You can also use a 9 by 13-inch baking dish and cut the cornbread into squares after it cools.

What You Need

2 mixing bowls   Whisk   12-cup muffin tin

How to Make

Preheat oven to 375F.

1. In a bowl, mix all the dry ingredients together.
2. In a separate bowl, whisk eggs and milk together; then fold into dry ingredients. Mix until smooth. Batter should have a thick consistency.
3. Add butter, oil, and jalapeño chile to the batter.
4. Spray muffin cups with PAM cooking spray and fill 3/4 full with batter.
5. Top each muffin with a sprinkle of cheese and bake until golden brown, about 20 minutes. Serve hot.

*See "diced" and "PAM cooking spray" in the Glossary.

Ingredients

1/2 cup yellow cornmeal
1-1/2 cups all-purpose white flour
1/2 cups granulated sugar
1 tablespoon baking powder
1/4 teaspoon ground cumin
1/2 teaspoon kosher salt
2 eggs
1-1/4 cups milk
3 tablespoons melted butter
1/3 cup vegetable oil
3 tablespoons finely diced* jalapeño chile
PAM cooking spray*
1/3 cup shredded cheddar cheese

POPOVERS

Makes 8 popovers

Fragrant, steaming popovers are a treat any time, but I particularly like them with brunch or as the centerpiece of a continental breakfast. Crisp on the outside, slightly chewy and airy in the middle, and slathered with butter and sweet preserves (strawberry's a good choice), these puffy puppies are an addictive treat. You may have to practice a little to get the rise just right. It's also important to make sure the centers are dry but not dried out. Once you've got the technique down, you can make these with ease and impress your friends and family.

What You Need

Mixing bowl   Whisk   Muffin tin or popover pan

How to Make

Preheat oven to 450F.

1. In the bowl, lightly whisk eggs and milk.
2. Add flour and salt and whisk just until smooth.
3. Let batter stand for 30 minutes.
4. Grease muffin cups and fill each halfway with batter.
5. Bake for 15 minutes. The popovers should be puffy at this point.
6. Turn down the heat to 350F and bake until popovers are brown and crisp, 15 to 20 minutes. For the last couple of minutes, leave the oven door ajar to release some of the heat and dry the centers of the popovers.
7. Serve hot.

Ingredients

2 eggs
1 cup milk
1 cup all-purpose flour
1/2 teaspoon salt

JICAMA-APPLE COLESLAW

Serves 4 to 6

Here's a refreshing twist on the usual coleslaw. Sweet, crunchy jicama and Fuji apples work well together to make this a favorite — and perhaps set a new gold standard for slaws. Add flavor by garnishing with orange segments and cilantro sprigs.

What You Need

Large bowl   Mandoline

How to Make

1. With the mandoline, very finely julienne* carrot, jicama, and apples.
2. Place in the bowl and mix well with cabbage, cider vinegar, sugar, and mayonnaise. Season with salt and pepper to taste.
3. Let sit for 15 minutes, to allow flavors to meld, and then serve.

*See "julienne" in the Glossary.

.

Ingredients

1 carrot, peeled
1 pound jicama
3 Fuji apples, peeled
1 green cabbage, shredded
1/4 cup apple cider vinegar
1/4 cup granulated sugar
1/3 cup mayonnaise
Salt and pepper

MEMPHIS COLESLAW

Serves 4 to 6

This coleslaw is a little more tart than is typical, with a bit of zingy spice as well. I like it on sandwiches, especially barbecued pulled pork. It also works well with seafood dishes such as fried catfish, seared scallops, and grilled mahi mahi.

What You Need

Mixing bowl   Box grater

How to Make

Grate carrots with the box grater. In the bowl, mix all ingredients together. Season with salt and pepper to taste and let sit for at least 15 minutes to allow flavors to meld before serving.

Ingredients

2 carrots, peeled
1 green cabbage, shredded
1/2 red onion, sliced thin
1 tablespoon Creole mustard
1 pinch cayenne pepper
1/3 cup sherry vinegar
1 tablespoon granulated sugar
Salt and pepper

BLACK BEANS

Serves 4 to 6

Fresh-cooked black beans make a big difference in any dish because they're so flavorful and have such a meaty texture. They don't take long to cook, and you can freeze them in small batches for later use. Freshly made beans are much tastier than canned beans, but if you must use canned, try organic whole beans.

For a simple and delicious soup, purée the beans with reduced chicken stock and top with Cotija cheese and salsa.

What You Need

Large stockpot   Colander   Food processor

How to Make

1. Pick through beans and discard any small stones and twigs that you find. Rinse beans well; then drain in the colander.
2. In the stockpot, add beans and 5 cups of water. Soak for at least 2 hours.
3. Turn heat to medium and add 5 cups water along with onion, cilantro, chili powder, and cumin.
4. Cook the beans at a low boil, stirring often from the bottom, for about 1 hour and 15 minutes to 1 hour and 30 minutes. Beans are done when they are soft but not mushy.
5. Remove from heat. Transfer about one-fourth of the beans to the food processor and carefully purée them with the olive oil.
6. Return bean purée to the pot and add salt to taste. Beans usually need a good amount of salt to enhance their flavor.
7. Transfer beans from the pot to a bowl to cool or top with cheese and serve.

*See "chop" and "dice" in the Glossary.

Ingredients

3 cups dried black beans
10 cups water
1 cup diced* yellow onion
1 bunch chopped* cilantro
1 teaspoon chili powder
1 teaspoon ground cumin
2 tablespoons extra-virgin
    olive oil
Salt
Shredded Cotija, jack, or
    cheddar cheese

PINTO BEANS

Serves 6 to 8

Pinto beans are the workhorse of the dried bean family. Russet-colored, meaty, and tender, these versatile beans enhance scores of savory dishes.

What You Need

4-quart stockpot   Colander

How to Make

1. Pick through beans and discard any small stones or twigs you find. Rinse thoroughly; then soak in 5 cups of water for 4 hours.
2. Drain beans in the colander. Put them in the stockpot with 8 cups water. Add garlic cloves and bacon (if using).
3. Bring to a boil; then turn heat to medium-low and cook until beans are tender, about 2 to 2-1/2 hours. Add salt to taste when done.

Ingredients

1 pound pinto beans
13 cups water
3 cloves garlic, peeled
1 thick piece bacon (optional)
Salt

ASIAN SOBA NOODLE SALAD

Serves 4 to 6

This side dish complements many types of foods. Serve with Hoisin Short Ribs (recipe, p. 123), Sweet Chili Pork Riblets (recipe, p. 125), or grilled fish. Soba is based on buckwheat, which makes it extra nutritious.

What You Need

5-quart stockpot   Large bowl   Strainer   Ice water

How to Make

1. In the stockpot, bring water to a boil. Cook noodles until al dente (follow directions on the package). Drain noodles in the strainer and then cool in ice water to prevent overcooking. Drain again.
2. Put the noodles in the bowl.
3. Add all the rest of the ingredients and toss gently and thoroughly with your hands.
4. Let sit for at least 1 hour so the flavors meld.
5. Garnish with toasted sesame seeds and cilantro sprigs (if using) and serve.

*See "chop," "dice," and "sambal" in the Glossary; for toasting, see Tips and Techniques.

Ingredients

2 pounds soba noodles (or angel hair pasta)

1/2 cup chopped* green onions, green and white parts

1/2 red onion, sliced thin

2 tablespoons peeled and finely chopped ginger

1 tablespoon peeled and finely chopped garlic

1/4 cup light soy sauce

1/4 cup hoisin

3 tablespoons honey

1/4 cup seasoned rice vinegar

1 fresh jalapeño chile, seeded and finely diced*

1 tablespoon sambal*

2 cups bean sprouts, rinsed and dried

1/8 cup sesame oil

1/8 cup canola oil

1/2 cup chopped cilantro

Toasted* sesame seeds and cilantro sprigs for garnish (optional)

MASHED POTATOES

Serves 8 to 10

This is one of the most popular dishes all over the world — any place where potatoes are grown. Like the perfect white shirt, mashed potatoes go with just about everything. You can make them mild or spicy, eat them piled on a plate with butter or gravy, form them into cakes, stuff them, turn them into pudding — anything goes. Think of this basic recipe as the starting point for hundreds of fun possibilities. (Tip: Cutting the potatoes into small cubes helps them cook evenly and release their starch more quickly.)

What You Need

4-quart stockpot   Colander   Potato whip

How to Make

1. In the stockpot, add cubed potatoes and enough water to cover. Add garlic.
2. Turn heat to medium high, bring to a boil, and cook until the potatoes fall apart when touched with a fork, about 20 minutes. Turn off heat.
3. Empty potatoes into the colander and drain. Put the drained potatoes back into the stockpot and add butter, milk, and salt.
4. With the whip, mix thoroughly. The potatoes should fluff right up. Serve immediately.

Ingredients

8 russet potatoes, peeled and cut into 1-inch cubes
4 garlic cloves, peeled
1/4 cup (1 stick) unsalted butter, at room temperature
1 cup milk
1 tablespoon salt

Try adding different flavorings to your mashed potatoes.

For roasted garlic mashed potatoes, add 3 tablespoons chopped roasted garlic.* For horseradish mashed potatoes, add 1 tablespoon prepared horseradish.

*For roasting garlic, see Tips and Techniques.

CREOLE POTATO SALAD

Serves 12 to 16

Transform the traditional potato salad by adding a little spice to it. The Creole touch makes this version a hit at potluck picnics, as a side dish for fried chicken, po' boy sandwiches, ribs, and barbecued chicken, or as a treat all by itself.

What You Need

8-quart stockpot   Colander   Large bowl

How to Make

1. In the stockpot, bring water to a boil. Add potatoes and boil until they're fork-tender.
2. Drain in the colander and let cool. Then peel and cut into 1-inch chunks.
3. In the bowl, combine potatoes with the rest of the ingredients, mix well, and season with salt and pepper to taste. Cover and refrigerate overnight for best flavor.

*See "chop" and "dice" in the Glossary.

Ingredients

12 large russet potatoes
1 yellow onion, finely diced*
1 bunch green onions, white and green parts, finely chopped*
2 green bell peppers, finely diced
2 red bell peppers, finely diced
3 tablespoons Creole mustard
1-1/3 cups mayonnaise
Pinch cayenne pepper
1/2 teaspoon paprika
2 tablespoons Worcestershire sauce
2 tablespoons Tabasco sauce
1/3 cup chopped Italian parsley
6 hardboiled eggs, coarsely chopped
1/3 cup pickle relish
1 tablespoon granulated sugar
2 tablespoons champagne vinegar
Salt and pepper

CITRUS FINGERLING POTATO SALAD

Serves 4

This potato salad is exceptionally light compared to the more traditional American versions made with mayonnaise. The orange zest adds a refreshing twist. For more color, replace some of the fingerlings with Peruvian purple potatoes.

What You Need

5-quart stockpot   Colander   Large bowl

How to Make

1. In the stockpot, bring water to a boil and add salt to taste. Add potatoes and boil until they're fork-tender.
2. Drain in the colander, let cool, and then slice lengthwise.
3. In the bowl, combine potatoes with the rest of the ingredients, cover, and refrigerate overnight.
4. Just before serving, cut each tomato into 10 wedges and toss into the salad.

*See "chop" and "dice" in the Glossary.

Ingredients

4 pounds fingerling potatoes
Salt
Zest of 2 oranges
Juice of 2 oranges
1 medium red onion, finely diced*
1/4 cup extra-virgin olive oil
1/4 cup champagne vinegar
2 tablespoons chopped* fresh tarragon
3 tablespoons chopped parsley
1 bunch chives, chopped
2 tablespoons granulated sugar
4 slices cooked bacon, finely chopped (optional)
2 tomatoes

POTATO CROQUETTES

Makes 16 to 20 croquettes

These tasty little morsels are a great way to use up leftover mashed potatoes. Serve them with chicken or beef or as an appetizer with a little Pesto (recipe, p. 235). You can also play around with the ingredients you use to flavor them.

What You Need

2 mixing bowls   Cookie sheet   12-inch deep-sided frying pan or deep-fryer
Rack

How to Make

1. In a bowl, mix Mashed Potatoes with prosciutto, mozzarella, Parmesan, chives, onions, salt, and pepper; then beat 1 egg into the mixture. Potatoes should be soft enough to shape.
2. In a bowl, mix 2 eggs well and set aside.
3. Take a generous tablespoon of the potatoes, about 1-1/4 ounces, and shape into a log about 1-1/2 inches thick and 3 inches long. Repeat until all the potatoes have been formed into croquettes.
4. Roll each croquette in flour, then dip into the beaten eggs, then roll in the panko bread crumbs, and then set on the cookie sheet. Repeat until all the croquettes are coated and breaded.
5. Refrigerate, covered, for at least 2 hours or overnight.
6. When ready to cook the croquettes, heat the frying pan over medium-high heat and melt the Crisco. It should be about 1/2 inch deep.
7. Gently lay the croquettes in the hot oil and fry* on all sides until golden brown, about 3 minutes per side. Remove to the rack to dry.
8. Keep warm in a very low oven (200F) until ready to serve.

*See "chop" and "Parmesan" in the Glossary; for frying, see Tips and Techniques.

Ingredients

3 to 4 cups chilled Mashed Potatoes (recipe, p. 191)
1/3 cup finely chopped* prosciutto
1 cup shredded mozzarella
1/2 cup grated Parmesan*
1/4 cup finely chopped chives
1/4 cup finely chopped yellow onion
Salt and pepper to taste
3 eggs
1 cup all-purpose flour
2 cups panko bread crumbs
1-1/2 cups Crisco or vegetable oil

POTATO-SPINACH GRATIN

Serves 8 to 10

Creamy, savory, and rich, this tender casserole is a cross between a vegetable torte and a classic French gratin. It's a versatile accompaniment to many dishes such as rack of lamb and grilled steaks or chicken.

You can also serve it as a vegetarian entrée paired with grilled portobello mushrooms, Roasted Tomatoes (recipe, p. 204), and balsamic reduction.

What You Need

Mandoline   9 x 13-inch glass baking dish   Cookie sheet

How to Make

Preheat oven to 375F.

1. With the mandoline, cut potatoes into slices 1/8-inch thick.
2. Spray the baking dish well with PAM cooking spray; then completely cover the bottom of the dish with a layer of potato slices. Pour on a little of the cream, season with a pinch of salt and pepper, and add some of the spinach, garlic, and shallots. Sprinkle with some of the Parmesan and Gruyère. Repeat until all the potatoes are used up, reserving some of the cream and cheeses.
3. Pour the reserved cream on top, sprinkle on a pinch of nutmeg, and cover with the reserved cheeses.
4. Place the cookie sheet on the rack below the baking dish in case the gratin bubbles over. Cover baking dish with foil and bake until fork-tender, about 1-1/2 hours.
5. When gratin is done, it will seem a little liquidy but will firm up as it cools.
6. For presenting on plates, allow to cool and then slice and reheat. For family-style service, dish it up straight from the oven, right out of the baking dish.

*See "chopped," "PAM cooking spray," and "Parmesan" in the Glossary; for blanching, see Tips and Techniques.

Ingredients

6 large russet potatoes, peeled
PAM cooking spray*
3 cups heavy cream
Salt and pepper
2 cups blanched,* chopped* spinach, with excess water squeezed out
2 tablespoons finely chopped garlic
3 tablespoons finely chopped shallots
3/4 cup grated Parmesan*
1-1/2 cups grated Gruyère or fontina cheese
Nutmeg

CRISPY POTATO HASH

Serves 4

Who doesn't love buttery, crunchy hash made with smooth, soft potatoes? It's a celebration of texture.

Always precook your breakfast potatoes, by either boiling or baking them before frying. That way, they become crisp, not starchy. You could even precook them the night before. Try using a mixture of different potatoes to give this dish a unique flavor. Feel free to improvise and use any kind of potato you like.

What You Need

Large frying pan   Wooden spoon

How to Make

1. Heat the frying pan over medium-high heat. Add oil and then potatoes.
2. With the wooden spoon, stir the potatoes; then let them sit until they start to brown, about 2 to 3 minutes.
3. Stir again and let brown some more, another 2 to 3 minutes.
4. Add onions, a pinch of cayenne pepper, garlic and onion powders, paprika, thyme, salt, and pepper. (Hint: A little more salt goes a long way when cooking potatoes.)
5. Continue to cook until potatoes are browned and crispy. Add butter at the end and serve piping hot.

*See "dice" in the Glossary.

Ingredients

1/4 cup canola oil
1 cup cooked, diced* russet potatoes (about 1 potato)
1 cup cooked, diced red potatoes (about 3 potatoes)
2 cups cooked, diced Yukon Gold potatoes (about 3 potatoes)
1/2 cup finely diced red onion
1/2 cup chopped green onion, both white and green parts
Cayenne pepper
1 tablespoon garlic powder
1 tablespoon onion powder
1 teaspoon paprika
1/2 teaspoon dried thyme
Salt and pepper to taste
2 tablespoons unsalted butter

CRISPY FRENCH FRIES

Serves 4 to 6

Making great French fries is much easier than most people think. The secret is to cook the potatoes twice and let them cool in between. That's what gives the outside a rich bronze crunch and makes the inside so smooth and tender. If you have a deep-fryer, it's a snap, but a frying pan and a thermometer will do the trick as well. It just takes a little time and practice.

Once you've mastered the basic fries, you're ready to try making Blue Cheese Fries, a Toast specialty.

(Remember, the oil gets extremely hot, so be very careful and do not allow children anywhere near the kitchen when you're frying.)

What You Need

Deep-fryer or 12-inch deep-sided frying pan, cooking thermometer, and strainer
Sheet pan

Ingredients

6 russet potatoes
Vegetable oil or peanut oil
Salt and pepper

How to Make

1. Peel potatoes, cut into 1/3-inch-wide strips, and soak in water overnight to remove the starch.
2. Drain the potatoes. In the deep-fryer, heat oil, enough to cover the potatoes, to 250F. Fry* potatoes in small batches, 2 minutes per batch. They should look pale and limp.
3. Lay out potatoes on the sheet pan and let cool. Make sure the oil returns to 250F before you add the next batch.
4. Refrigerate the partially cooked fries for at least 2 hours, so their internal temperature drops.
5. In the deep-fryer, heat oil to 350F and cook the fries in small batches until golden brown and crisp. Salt and pepper to taste and serve hot, fresh from the fryer.

Blue Cheese Fries

What You Need

Frying pan

How to Make

1. While the Crispy French Fries are still hot, melt butter in the frying pan over medium-high heat and add garlic.
2. Cook for 1 minute; then add the fries and toss with the butter by gently shaking the pan up and down.
3. While shaking the pan, sprinkle on the crumbled cheese and let it melt evenly on the fries.
4. Add parsley and serve immediately.

See "chop" in the Glossary; for frying, see Tips and Techniques.

Ingredients

3 cups freshly cooked Crispy French Fries
1 tablespoon unsalted butter
1 teaspoon chopped* garlic
3 tablespoons Maytag Blue Cheese, Point Reyes blue cheese, or Gorgonzola, crumbled into small bits
2 tablespoons chopped parsley

FRIED LEEKS

Makes 2 cups

This is an elegant yet simple side dish or garnish that enhances steaks and any fish or poultry dish. Use it to add flavor, depth, and just the right amount of texture for balancing out the main dish.

What You Need

12-inch deep-sided frying pan or deep-fryer   Skimmer

How to Make

1. Cut the leek in half lengthwise and then in half crosswise. Discard the dark green parts.
2. Wash well, making sure all sand and dirt are removed, and dry.
3. Finely julienne* the white and the light green parts of the leek. Toss leek strips in flour.
4. In the frying pan, heat oil to 325F and fry* leek strips until light brown and crispy.
5. With the skimmer, remove strips and let dry on a towel. Season with salt and pepper to taste.

*See "julienne" in the Glossary; for frying, see Tips and Techniques.

Ingredients

1 large leek
1/2 cup all-purpose flour
1/2 cup Crisco
Salt and pepper

ROASTED FENNEL BULBS

Makes 2 pounds

I'm always amazed by the way roasting transforms just about any food. Fennel bulbs come into their own when they are roasted, developing a velvety texture and anise nuances. They're particularly delicious with fish and chicken, as either an accompaniment or a garnish.

What You Need

Mixing bowl   Aluminum foil   Cookie sheet   Small bowl

How to Make

Preheat oven to 375F.

1. In the mixing bowl, toss fennel bulbs with olive oil, salt, and pepper.
2. Wrap each bulb in aluminum foil. Bake until each is soft to the touch, about 1 hour.
3. Remove from the foil and coarsely chop.*
4. Transfer the juices to the small bowl and reserve.

*See "chop" in the Glossary.

Ingredients

4 fennel bulbs, about 1/2 pound each
4 tablespoons olive oil
Salt and pepper to taste

ROASTED CAULIFLOWER WITH CAPER VINAIGRETTE

Serves 4

You'll be amazed by the way this simple side dish pops with flavor. It would be a fine accompaniment to an antipasti platter or grilled or roasted fish and even makes a savory snack. With roasting, the cauliflower develops a sweet, nutty taste that rounds out the tanginess of the capers. For even more flavor, add one or two finely minced anchovy fillets or sprinkle with chopped roasted hazelnuts. This dish is delicious hot or cold.

What You Need

Mixing bowl   Cookie sheet

How to Make

Preheat oven to 450F.

1. In the bowl, toss the cauliflower with 2 tablespoons of olive oil, salt, and pepper.
2. Lay out on the cookie sheet and roast until just softened and browned, about 15 to 20 minutes.
3. Remove to the bowl. Add 2 tablespoons olive oil and toss with capers, parsley, and sherry vinegar. Check for salt and pepper. Either chill and serve later or serve hot right away.

*See "chop" in the Glossary.

Ingredients

1 head cauliflower, cut into small wedges, with core intact
4 tablespoons olive oil
Salt and pepper to taste
1 tablespoon capers, coarsely chopped*
3 tablespoons finely chopped Italian parsley
2 tablespoons sherry vinegar

ROASTED JALAPEÑOS

Makes 12 roasted chiles

Roasting intensifies both the flavor and the heat of jalapeño chiles. I marinate them afterward with a touch of vinegar and use them as a side dish or a garnish with many dishes and sandwiches. Just be sure to remind your guests that the chiles can be hot! You could also use a grill to coax out a smoky flavor. Grill the jalapeños just enough to mark, not char, them and then finish up in the oven.

(Important: Use gloves whenever you work with chiles. And be especially careful not to touch your eyes or face.)

What You Need

2 mixing bowls   Cookie sheet

Ingredients

12 fresh jalapeño chiles
2 tablespoons olive oil
Salt and pepper to taste
5 cloves garlic, peeled and
   sliced thin
1/2 yellow onion, sliced thin
1/4 cup rice vinegar
1 tablespoon granulated sugar

How to Make

Preheat oven to 500F.

1. In a bowl, toss jalapeños with olive oil, salt, and pepper.
2. Lay chiles on the cookie sheet, making sure there's space around each one. Roast in the oven until they start to shrivel and brown lightly, about 15 to 18 minutes.
3. Remove from oven and let cool.
4. In a bowl, mix garlic, onion, vinegar, and sugar.
5. Toss the jalapeños in the dressing and then refrigerate. Roasted jalapeños will keep in the refrigerator for about a week.

ROASTED TOMATOES

Serves 8 to 10

I love the rich, bright, mellow character of roasted tomatoes. They add depth to savory dishes, and their ruby-red color makes them a terrific garnish or side dish. Plus, they're a snap to make.

What You Need

Mixing bowl   Cookie sheet

How to Make

Preheat oven to 375F.

1. Cut tomatoes lengthwise and squeeze out the seeds. Place in the bowl.
2. Add garlic, basil, oregano, salt, pepper, and olive oil and toss gently.
3. Place tomatoes cut side up on the cookie sheet. Bake for 15 minutes.

*See "chop" in the Glossary.

Ingredients

10 Roma tomatoes
1 tablespoon chopped* garlic
1 teaspoon basil
1 teaspoon oregano
Salt and pepper to taste
4 tablespoons olive oil

HUSH PUPPIES

Serves 4

In the early days of the American South, when every family hunted and kept packs of dogs, little bits of deep-fried cornmeal batter were frequently tossed to the barking dogs to quiet them, along with the shout, "Hush, puppies." Forever after, the crunchy, fragrant little rounds of fried cornmeal dough were known by the affectionate name "hush puppies." They'll certainly quiet any hungry person and put a smile on just about anyone's face.

What You Need

Deep-sided frying pan   Cooking thermometer   Mixing bowl
Tablespoon   Slotted spoon

How to Make

1. In the frying pan, add oil to a depth of about 1/2 inch. Heat oil to 350F, checking the temperature with the cooking thermometer.
2. In the bowl, combine the rest of the ingredients and mix until blended into a smooth batter.
3. Using a tablespoon, scoop up batter and carefully drop into the hot oil. Repeat a few more times, making sure not to crowd the spoonfuls of batter.
4. Fry* each hush puppy on one side for 1 minute; then turn over and cook for 1 minute more until golden brown. Remove with the slotted spoon and let drain on a towel. Repeat until all the batter is used. Serve hot.

*For frying, see Tips and Techniques.

Ingredients

Vegetable oil
1 cup yellow cornmeal
1/2 cup flour
1-1/2 teaspoons baking powder
1 teaspoon salt
1 teaspoon granulated sugar
1/4 teaspoon garlic powder
1/4 teaspoon pepper
1 egg, beaten
1/4 cup milk
3/4 cup minced onions

DESSERTS

DESSERTS

Who doesn't love a flavorful dessert that rounds out a meal with a memorable sweet finish? I call the desserts assembled here "cooks' desserts," because they're quick and easy and you don't have to be a pastry chef to make them. Just have fun with these recipes, and try a few variations once you become comfortable with them.

PROFITEROLES

Makes 16 2-1/2-inch puffs

Profiteroles — cream puffs stuffed with ice cream and drizzled with sauce — are among the most versatile of all desserts. They can be prepared in many different ways, which is a large part of their charm. In this recipe, they're stuffed with hazelnut gelato and topped with chocolate and caramel sauces. You could also fill them with whipped cream, like a cream puff, or with different custards. By the way, a cake decorated with custard-filled profiteroles makes for an impressive presentation.

What You Need

4-quart saucepan   Electric hand-held mixer or whisk   Cookie sheet
Wax paper   1-1/2-ounce ice cream scoop

How to Make

Preheat oven to 400F.

1. In the saucepan, bring water, butter, and salt to a boil over medium-high heat.
2. Mix in flour, incorporating thoroughly until the mixture starts to pull away from the edges of the pan.
3. Pull off heat. With the electric mixer, beat in eggs one at a time until the mixture forms a pasty dough. It should be shiny.
4. With the ice cream scoop, scoop out dough and drop on a cookie sheet lined with wax paper. Make sure the balls are at least 2 inches apart.
5. Bake for 20 minutes; then turn heat down to 325F and bake until the puffs are browned and feel light and airy, not heavy or moist in the middle, about 25 minutes.
6. Remove from oven and let cool for a few minutes.
7. Cut each puff in half horizontally and place a small scoop of gelato on the bottom half. Cover with the top half.
8. Arrange on a platter or on individual plates. Drizzle with caramel and chocolate sauces. Finish with a dab of whipped cream and sprinkle with toasted hazelnuts. Serve immediately, before it melts.

*For fresh whipped cream and toasting, see Tips and Techniques.

Ingredients

2 cups water
1 cup (2 sticks) unsalted butter
1/3 teaspoon kosher salt
2 cups flour
8 extra-large eggs
1 quart hazelnut gelato
1/2 cup of your favorite store-bought chocolate sauce
1/2 cup of your favorite store-bought caramel sauce
1 cup fresh whipped cream*
1/2 cup chopped toasted* hazelnuts

LAVENDER CRÈME BRÛLÉE

Serves 4

Here's a sensuous, aromatic little twist to traditional crème brûlée — finely chopped dried lavender, which gives this rich custard a summery edge. Dress it up by garnishing with sugar cookies, a little whipped cream, fresh berries, and a dusting of powdered sugar. The recipe also works as a base for other types of flavored brûlées. Just omit the lavender and substitute a little pumpkin purée, cocoa powder, shredded coconut, or fresh raspberries or blueberries, whatever your taste buds desire.

What You Need

2-quart saucepan   Mixing bowl   Strainer   Whisk   Sheet pan or roasting pan
4 4-ounce ramekins

How to Make

Preheat oven to 350F.

1. In the saucepan, heat cream, vanilla, and lavender over medium heat until mixture just begins to steam.
2. In the mixing bowl, whip egg yolks with sugar and a pinch of salt.
3. Slowly pour hot cream through the strainer into the eggs, whisking continuously. Skim off bubbles.
4. Ladle about 4 ounces into each of four ramekins.
5. Place ramekins on the sheet pan. Add water to the pan, enough to reach one-quarter to halfway up the ramekins.
6. Bake until the middle of the custards are set, about 25 minutes.
7. Remove from oven. Let cool; then refrigerate overnight.
8. Sprinkle some sugar on top of each custard. Place the ramekins under a broiler, within an inch of the flame, and broil just until the sugar caramelizes.

Ingredients

2 cups heavy cream
1-1/2 tablespoons pure vanilla extract
1 teaspoon chopped dried lavender
Yolks of 5 extra-large eggs
1/3 cup granulated sugar plus more for caramelizing
Salt

POLENTA PUDDING

Serves 6 to 8

Rich with golden corn flavor and studded with fresh summer fruits, this unique pudding is a wonderful choice for breakfast or brunch on a warm summer day. I like to serve it chilled, in cup-shaped bowls, topped with a dollop of whipped cream. Accompany the pudding with an iced latte and fresh-baked bread with ricotta-honey spread.

What You Need

4-quart saucepan   6- to 8-ounce serving bowls

How to Make

1. In the saucepan, combine milk, half and half, butter, sugar, and a pinch of salt over medium heat. Stir.
2. When mixture begins to heat up, add polenta, stirring constantly until it begins to thicken, about 4 to 5 minutes.
3. Lower heat to a simmer* and add Grand Marnier, a pinch of cinnamon, orange zest, a pinch of nutmeg, and raisins.
4. Cook for about 10 more minutes, remove from heat, and add peaches, blueberries, plums, and apricots.
5. Carefully ladle into bowls. Let cool to room temperature, about 30 minutes; then refrigerate overnight.
6. Garnish with lightly sweetened fresh whipped cream just before serving.

*See "simmer" in the Glossary; for fresh whipped cream, see Tips and Techniques.

Ingredients

3 cups milk
1-1/2 cups half and half
2 tablespoons butter
7 tablespoons granulated sugar
Salt
3/4 cup coarse-ground polenta
2 tablespoons Grand Marnier
    or other orange liqueur
Cinnamon
1/2 teaspoon orange zest
Nutmeg
3 tablespoons raisins
3 peaches, peeled and sliced
1/4 cup blueberries
2 plums, pitted and sliced
3 apricots, pitted and sliced
Fresh whipped cream*

CINNAMON APPLE FRITTERS

Serves 4 to 6

This dessert is not only scrumptious but also so much easier to make than you might think. Fuji or Golden Delicious apples are good choices for this recipe. The hot fritters and cold ice cream delight the palate with their crispy and creamy textures.

What You Need

Mixing bowl   Deep-fryer or 12-inch deep-sided frying pan, preferably cast iron, and candy thermometer   Skewer   Large bowl

How to Make

1. In the mixing bowl, combine flour, rice flour, egg, baking powder, buttermilk, water, sugar, and a pinch of salt. Mix well and let rest for 1 hour. The batter should be thick, almost doughy.
2. Mix apples with batter. Mixture should be mostly apples, coated with just a little batter so that the pieces cling together. Add 1 tablespoon of cinnamon and mix.
3. In the deep-fryer, heat Crisco to 375F. When oil reaches the right temperature, drop in tablespoon-size lumps of battered apples. They should start frying instantly.
4. Turn fritters as they brown. When browned on both sides, poke with a skewer to see if they are done. The skewer should be wet but have no trace of batter.
5. Remove fritters and place on towels to drain.
6. Place fritters in the large bowl, add honey and 1 tablespoon cinnamon, and toss.
7. Put 2 or 3 fritters on a plate along with a scoop of ice cream. Serve immediately.

*See "dice" in the Glossary.

Ingredients

1-1/2 cups all-purpose flour
1/2 cup rice flour
1 egg
1-1/2 teaspoons baking powder
1 cup buttermilk
1/3 cup water
1 tablespoon granulated sugar
Salt
3 apples, diced*
2 tablespoons cinnamon
1 cup Crisco
3 tablespoons honey
Vanilla ice cream

RICOTTA CHEESE TORTE
WITH BRANDIED NECTARINES

Makes 1 10-inch torte

Light and moist, with the tangy sweetness of nectarines to balance the delicate cheese flavor, this homey dessert is ideal for a summer dinner party — or just for the family. It's all about simple fresh ingredients and pretty presentation. You can substitute other fruits for the nectarines, such as fresh figs when they are in season, but I think this combination presents nectarines at their ripest, golden best.

   (Note: The recipe for brandied nectarines makes enough for four slices of torte. If serving more, just increase the amounts accordingly.)

What You Need

2 mixing bowls   Wooden spoon or hand-held mixer   9-inch springform pan
Cooling rack   3-quart saucepan   Whisk

How to Make

Preheat oven to 350F.

1. In a mixing bowl, combine 1 cup softened butter with 1-1/4 cups of sugar using the wooden spoon until they're fully blended and form soft mounds.
2. Add eggs, egg yolk, milk, and 1/2 cup of ricotta and mix well until blended.
3. Slowly add flour, baking powder, a pinch of salt, vanilla, and orange zest, mixing just until all ingredients are thoroughly incorporated. Do not overbeat.
4. Pour batter into greased 9-inch springform pan. Bake until middle is firm and bouncy, about 45 to 50 minutes. Let cool; then remove from pan and finish cooling on the rack.
5. In the saucepan, reduce* 1/4 cup sugar and 1/2 cup water to a thick syrup over medium-high heat.
6. Add nectarines and peach brandy. When brandy hits the hot pan, it will flame for a few seconds. Don't be alarmed, but do stand back.
7. When flames die down, add butter and sauté* nectarines for no more than 1 minute. You don't want to cook the nectarines, just sweeten them in the syrup without making them mushy.
8. In a mixing bowl, fold 4 tablespoons ricotta into the whipped cream with the whisk.
9. Place a slice of torte on each of four plates. Top each serving with one-quarter of the brandied nectarines plus a dollop of the cream-and-ricotta mixture. Serve immediately.

*See "reduce" and "sauté" in the Glossary; for fresh whipped cream, see Tips and Techniques.

Ingredients

1 cup (2 sticks) unsalted butter, softened, plus 1 tablespoon unsalted butter
1-1/2 cups granulated sugar
3 extra-large eggs
1 egg yolk
1 cup milk
1/2 cup plus 4 tablespoons ricotta
2 cups cake flour
1 tablespoon baking powder
Salt
1 teaspoon pure vanilla extract
1 tablespoon orange zest
1/2 cup water
4 ripe nectarines, thinly sliced
2 ounces peach brandy
1/2 cup fresh whipped cream*

BRIOCHE BREAD PUDDING

Serves 6 to 8

Here's an extremely easy bread pudding for the home cook. It takes just a few minutes to prepare, not including baking time, and is delicious topped with your favorite ice cream, a little whipped cream, and fresh berries. This recipe lends itself to many variations as well. Try making it with different flavors of ice cream. Add chocolate chips or crushed Heath bars, coconut, cinnamon — you name it. Once you get the basic recipe down, it's easy to be creative and have fun.

What You Need

Mixing bowl   Whisk   1 large loaf pan   1 glass baking dish

How to Make

Preheat oven to 350F.

1. In the oven, lightly toast the bread cubes.
2. Place ice cream in the mixing bowl and allow to melt at room temperature.
3. Whip melted ice cream with eggs, egg yolk, milk, sugar, vanilla, and a pinch of salt.
4. Lay bread cubes in the ice cream mixture and soak for at least 1 hour.
5. Coat the loaf pan with PAM cooking spray and gently push the bread mixture into it.
6. Set the loaf pan inside the larger baking dish. Fill the baking dish with water until it reaches about halfway up the sides of the loaf pan.
7. Cover both pan and dish with foil and bake until the center of the pudding is stiff, about 1-1/2 hours.
8. Remove from oven and let rest for about 1 hour.
9. Cut into 8 equal pieces and serve.

*See "PAM cooking spray" in the Glossary.

Ingredients

1 loaf brioche bread, crusts trimmed, cut into 1-inch cubes (about 2 quarts of bread)

3-1/2 cups vanilla ice cream (I recommend Breyers Natural Vanilla)

2 eggs

1 egg yolk

2 cups milk

1 cup granulated sugar

1 tablespoon pure vanilla extract

Kosher salt

PAM cooking spray*

GARNISHES AND ACCENTS

BASIL OIL

Makes 2 cups

Use this oil to add a light basil flavor and beautiful green color. It's ideal as a garnish for soups or savory dishes.

What You Need

Blender   Saucepan   Ice water   Fine-mesh strainer   Small jar

How to Make

1. In the saucepan, bring water to a rapid boil. Add 1 tablespoon of salt. Blanch* basil for a few seconds; then plunge into ice water. Remove, squeeze out excess water with towels, and then rough-chop.* You should have about 1-1/2 cups.
2. Put chopped basil in the blender along with the olive oil, canola oil, and a pinch of salt. Blend for at least 2 minutes.
3. Let stand at least 3 hours; then pour through the strainer into the jar. Well-strained basil oil should last for about 3 to 4 weeks in the refrigerator.

*See "chop" in the Glossary; for blanching, see Tips and Techniques.

Ingredients

2 bunches fresh basil
Salt
1/2 cup olive oil
1 cup canola oil

CANDIED WALNUTS

Makes 2 cups

These always come in handy. I like to use them on salads or desserts, as a snack, or as an accompaniment for fruit and cheese. They're crunchy and sweet, with just a hint of spice — rather addictive! Try this recipe with other nuts or add different seasonings, such as rosemary, lavender, or vanilla.

What You Need

Nonreactive saucepan   Wooden spoon   Cookie sheet   Metal spatula

How to Make

Preheat oven to 325F.

1. Taste a few walnuts to make sure they're sweet, not bitter. Coat the cookie sheet with PAM cooking spray. Set aside.
2. In the saucepan, combine sugars and water and reduce* to a syrup over medium-high heat, about 4 minutes. The syrup should be fairly thick, like honey.
3. Add walnuts and stir with the wooden spoon, coating them all evenly. Be careful — the syrup will be extremely hot.
4. Lay out nuts on the cookie sheet. Sprinkle with salt and pepper to taste and a pinch of cayenne.
5. Bake until the sugar melts and browns, about 10 to 12 minutes. Keep an eye on the nuts to make sure they don't burn.
6. Remove from oven and let cool on the sheet; then scrape off with a metal spatula. The nuts will keep for a couple of weeks in an airtight container.

*See "PAM cooking spray" and "reduce" in the Glossary.

Ingredients

1 pound walnut halves and
    pieces
1/2 cup granulated sugar
1/4 cup brown sugar
3/4 cup water
PAM cooking spray*
Salt and pepper
Cayenne pepper

CARAMELIZED ONIONS

Makes 1 cup

Slow and steady is the way to make beautifully caramelized onions. Done right, they'll reward you with their surprising tender sweetness.

What You Need

4-quart saucepan   Wooden spoon

How to Make

1. In the saucepan, melt butter over medium-low heat.
2. Add onions, salt, and pepper and cook slowly, stirring often with the wooden spoon, until the onions become really soft and richly brown, about 15 to 20 minutes. If they darken too fast, lower the heat.

*See "chop" in the Glossary.

Ingredients

3 tablespoons unsalted butter
2 large yellow onions, roughly chopped*
Salt and pepper to taste

CROSTINI AND CROUTONS

Crunchy, crusty crostini and croutons add so much character to soups and salads, especially when they're made fresh and served warm. The trick is to keep your oven at 325F so that the bread gets thoroughly toasted and crisp without over-browning.

 Crostini are thin slices of toasted bread. Croutons are large-diced or hand-torn pieces. The inside of day-old French or sourdough bread makes the best croutons.

What You Need

Bowl   Baking sheet

How to Make

Preheat oven to 325F.

1. In the bowl, mix olive oil with garlic, basil, and salt.
2. Brush each crostini with seasoned oil on one side or gently toss croutons in the oil.
3. Place bread on the baking sheet and sprinkle with Parmesan and a pinch of pepper.
4. Bake until crisp and golden brown, about 12 to 15 minutes.

*See "chop" and "Parmesan" in the Glossary.

Ingredients

12 slices of baguette, cut diagonally, about 4 inches long and no more than 1/4 inch wide (for crostini)

2 cups hand-torn bread (for croutons)

1/3 cup olive oil

1 tablespoon chopped* garlic

2 tablespoons finely chopped fresh basil

1/2 teaspoon salt

1/3 cup grated Parmesan*

Freshly ground black pepper

FRIED FRESH HERBS

Fried herbs are always a nice garnish for entrées and soups. They're easy to make and can be prepared in advance. Basil and sage are two of my favorites for frying, but you can try this technique with other leafy herbs, such as Italian parsley, lavender leaves, and tarragon.

What You Need

2-quart deep-fryer or 5-quart pot and cooking thermometer   Mesh spoon

Ingredients

1 cup fresh basil or sage leaves
Canola oil
Salt

How to Make

1. Carefully wash basil or sage leaves; then pat dry with towels and separate the leaves.
2. In the deep-fryer, add enough oil to reach a depth of 3/4 inch and heat to 350F. (If frying* the herbs in the pot, check the oil temperature with the cooking thermometer.) Place the leaves directly into the oil. Be careful, because moisture in the leaves will cause the oil to splatter. Cook until crispy, about 30 to 40 seconds.
3. Remove with the mesh spoon and place in a single layer on a towel to drain. Season with a little salt to taste.

*For frying, see Tips and Techniques.

FRIED ONIONS

Who doesn't love the flavor boost fried onions bring to a hamburger, mashed potatoes, or a savory salad? They're amazingly versatile as well as easy to make.

What You Need

Mixing bowl   Mandoline   Frying basket   Tongs   Mesh spoon
2-quart deep-fryer or 5-quart pot, cooking thermometer, and strainer

How to Make

1. In the bowl, mix flour with paprika, garlic powder, 1/2 teaspoon salt, and pepper. Set aside.
2. With the mandoline, carefully slice the onion into very thin rings.
3. Toss onion rings thoroughly in seasoned flour.
4. In the deep-fryer, add enough oil to slightly cover the onions and heat to 350F. (If frying* the onions in the pot, check the oil temperature with the cooking thermometer.) Shake excess flour off onion rings and place a small batch of onions in the frying basket. With the tongs, stir the onions a little so they don't clump up. Fry until golden brown and crispy, about 1 to 1-1/2 minutes.
5. With a mesh spoon, remove onions and place in a single layer on towels to drain. Add a pinch more salt.
6. Repeat with another small batch of onions until all onions are done.

*For frying, see Tips and Techniques.

Ingredients

1-1/2 cups flour
1 teaspoon paprika
1 tablespoon garlic powder
1/2 teaspoon salt plus more to taste
1/3 teaspoon ground black pepper
1 large yellow onion
Vegetable oil

STOCKS, SAUCES, SALSAS

BASIC DEMI-GLACE

Makes 1 quart

Demi-glace, a rich, savory meat concentrate that enhances gravies, sauces, and a multitude of other dishes, is one of the most useful sauces to have in your repertoire. It does take a couple of days to prepare, but look on the bright side — you can freeze it in small amounts and have some ready to use whenever you need it.

In this recipe, I use veal bones, which you can obtain from the butcher. Beef bones work, too, but veal bones produce a much richer taste. Adding the herbs at the very end prevents them from turning the sauce bitter and keeps their flavors fresh. The red wine in my demi-glace contributes a deeper layer of flavor, but if you prefer to omit it, the recipe works beautifully without it.

What You Need

Roasting pan   8-quart stockpot   Fine-mesh strainer   Large storage container
Glass or ceramic casserole

How to Make

FOR THE VEAL STOCK:

Preheat oven to 400F.

1. In the roasting pan, lay out the bones in one even layer if possible.
2. Roast until the bones have turned a rich brown color.
3. In the stockpot, place bones and drippings from the roasting pan. Add onions, carrots, celery, leek, bay leaves, peppercorns, and water.
4. Bring to a boil; then turn down heat and cook at a very low simmer* for 4 hours. If the liquid reduces by half, add a little more water.
5. Pour the stock through the strainer into the container. Cool; then cover and refrigerate overnight.

Ingredients

For the veal stock (makes about 3 quarts):

5 pounds veal bones (ask the butcher to crack for you)
2 onions, peeled and quartered
2 carrots, peeled and chopped*
3 stalks celery, chopped
1 leek, chopped and washed
2 bay leaves
1 tablespoon black peppercorns
5 quarts cold water

For the demi-glace:

3 quarts veal stock
4 cups red wine (of a quality you'd like to drink)
5 shallots, peeled and halved
1 bay leaf
1 carrot, peeled and chopped
1 celery stalk, chopped
1 sprig fresh rosemary
1 sprig fresh thyme

FOR THE DEMI-GLACE:

1. Skim all the fat off the top of the refrigerated stock. The fat will have congealed into a white layer, so it should be easy to remove.
2. In the stockpot, add wine, shallots, and bay leaf and reduce* over medium heat by one-third.
3. Add the stock, carrot, and celery. Bring to a boil; then turn down to a high simmer.
4. Cook for about 1-1/2 hours or until reduced by two-thirds. Continue to skim off any fat while demi-glace is reducing.
5. Pull off heat. Add rosemary and thyme and steep the herbs for about 10 minutes.
6. Pour demi-glace through the strainer into the casserole. Cool; then cover and refrigerate overnight.
7. The next day, it should be hard and gelatinous. Remove any fat that has solidified on the top. Cut the demi-glace into large cubes, wrap individually, and freeze.

*See "chop," "reduce," and "simmer" in the Glossary.

BASIC HOLLANDAISE

Makes 2 cups

Using this recipe as a base, you will be able to create béarnaise sauce, chipotle hollandaise, dill hollandaise, roasted red pepper hollandaise — the list is almost endless.

The first step is to master basic hollandaise sauce. You could make it the traditional way and whisk it over a double boiler, but there's an easier, much quicker way for the home cook. Try this out and see how easy it is.

What You Need

2 microwave-safe containers (1 clear)   Food processor

How to Make

1. Place butter in a clear microwave-safe container such as a measuring cup. Microwave until butter is completely melted but does not boil. Set aside.
2. Put egg yolks in a microwave-safe container and lightly warm them for only a few seconds or until the edges are just starting to cook.
3. Place warmed egg yolks in the food processor; then turn it on and add lemon juice, Worcestershire sauce, Tabasco sauce, a tiny pinch of cayenne, and salt.
4. While the food processor is running, slowly drizzle in the butter. You will notice that the butterfat has formed a layer on top, leaving a milky liquid layer below. Keep your eye on the layers as you drizzle the melted butter into the food processor and stop pouring before you reach the liquid. Do your best to pour only the top layer of fat into the food processor. It will combine with the egg yolks and seasonings to yield a light, emulsified sauce that should coat the back of a spoon.
5. If the hollandaise is too thick, add a little hot water and pulse in the food processor. Salt to taste.
6. Spoon the warm sauce into a serving dish and keep in a warm place. (Don't let it get hot, as heat could cause the emulsion to separate.) The hollandaise will keep for up to 1 hour.

Ingredients

1 pound (4 sticks) plus
   3 tablespoons unsalted butter
5 egg yolks
1 tablespoon lemon juice
1 teaspoon Worcestershire
   sauce
1 teaspoon Tabasco sauce
Cayenne pepper
Salt to taste

CHAMPAGNE VINAIGRETTE

Makes 2 cups

This basic vinaigrette is indispensable — quite a few of the recipes in this book use it. It's also a good starting point for many variations. Try replacing the champagne vinegar with red wine, sherry, apple cider, or even a flavored vinegar. Add dill or tarragon, whole-grain mustard, or truffle oil.

I use a light salad oil because it makes a more delicate dressing that allows the flavors of the salad ingredients to shine through. But if you want to use olive oil, try 1 part olive oil to 2 parts salad oil, so the taste won't be overpowering.

What You Need

Food processor or mixing bowl and whisk

How to Make

1. In the food processor, add the vinegar, shallots, and honey. (If you don't have a food processor, blend the ingredients in the mixing bowl with the whisk.)
2. With the food processor running, slowly drizzle in the oil until the dressing is well blended and emulsified.
3. Add salt and pepper to taste. The dressing will keep for about a week in the refrigerator.

*See "chop" in the Glossary.

Ingredients

1/2 cup champagne vinegar
2 tablespoons chopped* shallots
1-1/2 tablespoons honey
1-1/2 cups canola oil
Salt and pepper

MEAT GRAVY FOR BISCUITS AND GRAVY

Makes enough for 10 biscuits

Just thinking about this classic gravy spooned over Buttermilk Biscuits (recipe, p. 182) and sprinkled with chopped green onions is enough to warm you up. There's a lot of meat in my version, but you can play around with the ingredients. If you make it ahead of time and freeze it in small batches, you'll have some ready when you need it.

What You Need

4-quart saucepan

How to Make

1. In the saucepan, melt butter over medium-high heat. Add bacon, sausages, chorizo, and onions and cook until all meat is browned, about 5 minutes.
2. Add Cajun spices, bay leaf, and thyme and cook for another minute.
3. Add flour and mix well. Make sure it blends smoothly with the meat and onions.
4. Add milk and stir in well.
5. Add salt to taste (or chicken base if using). Keep cooking, stirring from the bottom of the pan so the gravy doesn't burn as it thickens.
6. Add a splash of sherry (if using), Tabasco sauce to taste, Worcestershire sauce, and pepper to taste and check for salt. If gravy is too thick, add a little more milk.
7. Spoon immediately over split hot biscuits.

*See "chop" and "dice" in the Glossary.

Ingredients

2 tablespoons unsalted butter
1/4 cup chopped* bacon
1/2 cup chopped pork or chicken apple breakfast sausage
1/4 cup bulk mild Italian sausage
1/4 cup chorizo
1/2 cup diced* yellow onions
1 teaspoon Cajun spices
1 bay leaf
1/2 teaspoon chopped fresh thyme
5 tablespoons flour
3 cups milk
Salt and pepper
1 tablespoon concentrated no-MSG chicken base (optional)
Tabasco sauce
1 teaspoon Worcestershire sauce
Dry sherry (optional)

HOISIN SAUCE

Makes about 2 cups

This sweet-savory sauce is the basis for many Asian-inspired recipes and adds a piquant accent to other dishes as well. I love painting it on grilled poultry and meats and then caramelizing the sauce by finishing the meats on the grill.

What You Need

Food processor

How to Make

In the food processor, blend all ingredients well.

See "chop" and "sambal" in the Glossary.

Ingredients

1 cup hoisin (available in supermarkets or Asian grocery stores)

1/3 cup plum sauce (available in supermarkets or Asian grocery stores)

2 tablespoons peeled, chopped* ginger

1 tablespoon chopped garlic

2 tablespoons sambal*

1/2 cup orange juice

1 green onion, white and green parts, chopped

HOMEMADE CHICKEN STOCK

Makes 5 quarts

This chicken stock is easy to make even though it takes a little time. You can also make a dark chicken stock, which is a little richer and ideal for sauces, gravies, and some soups, by roasting the chicken bones until they're dark brown before making the stock. I favor a light chicken stock because its milder flavor makes it more versatile. Freeze the stock in small batches so you'll have some on hand when you need it.

What You Need

8- to 10-quart stockpot   Strainer   Large storage container

How to Make

1. In the stockpot, add all the ingredients and bring to a boil. Turn down heat to medium-low and simmer* for at least 3 hours. Or, if you have the time, turn the heat down very low and slow-simmer for much longer, which will really intensify the flavor.
2. Strain well into a large container and let cool to room temperature.
3. Refrigerate overnight, uncovered. The next day, remove the fat that has congealed on top of the stock.

*See "chop" and "simmer" in the Glossary.

Ingredients

5 pounds chicken bones, without skin (ask the butcher to save these for you)
7 quarts water
2 yellow onions, chopped*
4 carrots, peeled and chopped
1 leek, split and thoroughly washed (optional)
5 stalks celery, chopped
3 cloves garlic, peeled
1 bay leaf
1 teaspoon black peppercorns

PESTO

Makes 2 cups

Everybody needs to know how to make a simple pesto, and this is my favorite recipe based on fresh basil. Traditionally, pesto is made with a mortar and pestle, because hand-crushing releases the oils from the basil leaves, nuts, and garlic slowly, for maximum flavor, but a food processor also does a great job of blending the ingredients into a slightly rough paste.

What You Need

1-quart mortar and pestle

How to Make

In the mortar, use a rolling motion to crush half the ingredients with the pestle until they start to form a rough paste. Then add the rest of the ingredients and continue to crush and roll until all ingredients have become a rough paste.

*See "Grana Padano" and "Parmesan" in the Glossary; for toasting, see Tips and Techniques.

Ingredients

2 cups packed basil leaves, cleaned

1/2 cup toasted* pine nuts

5 garlic cloves, peeled, bottoms trimmed

3/4 cup olive oil

1/2 cup grated Parmesan* or Grana Padano*

1 tablespoon kosher salt

RANCHERO SAUCE

Makes about 1-1/2 quarts

This multipurpose sauce enhances a variety of dishes. On huevos rancheros, spinach Spanish omelets, and steaks, as a base for sautéing prawns, as a topping for burritos — these are just a few of the many ways to use ranchero sauce. Make it as spicy or mild as you wish by changing the amount of jalapeño chile you use. To store, let sauce cool to room temperature and then pour into smaller containers and freeze.

What You Need

4-quart deep-sided saucepan

How to Make

1. In the saucepan, add oil and sauté* onions, green pepper, jalapeño and chipotle chiles, cumin, ancho chile powder, paprika, and a pinch of oregano over medium-high heat until onions are translucent, about 5 to 8 minutes.
2. Add whole and crushed tomatoes, roasted red peppers, bay leaf, and water.
3. Bring to a boil; then turn down heat and simmer* until sauce is reduced* and thick in texture, about 1 hour. Make sure to stir from the bottom while it is reducing.
4. Remove bay leaf. Add salt, pepper, and a dash of hot sauce to taste. Serve hot.

*See "Cholula hot sauce," "chop," "dice," "reduce," "sauté," and "simmer" in the Glossary; for roasting peppers, see Tips and Techniques.

Ingredients

2 tablespoons olive oil
1 small yellow onion, finely diced*
1/2 cup diced green bell pepper
2 Roasted Jalapeños (recipe, p. 203), seeded and chopped* (use less if you prefer a milder sauce)
1 small chipotle chile
1 teaspoon ground cumin
1 tablespoon ancho chile powder
1 teaspoon smoked or regular paprika
Dried oregano
3 28-ounce cans whole peeled tomatoes, chopped
1 28-ounce can crushed tomatoes
1/2 cup chopped roasted red peppers*
1 bay leaf
1 cup water
Salt and pepper to taste
Cholula hot sauce*

ROASTED TOMATO COMPOTE

Makes 1-1/2 cups

Roasted Roma tomatoes are pure gold when they star in this flavorful compote. This versatile condiment will dress up fish, eggs, beef, sandwiches — literally any savory dish you can think of.

What You Need

12-inch sauté pan

How to Make

1. In the sauté pan, add 1 tablespoon of olive oil. Turn heat to high. When oil is hot, quickly sweat* the onions, about 3 minutes.
2. Add tomatoes and sauté* with garlic, curry powder, a pinch of sugar, and vinegar for about 10 minutes.
3. Add 1 tablespoon olive oil along with salt and pepper to taste.

*See "chop," "dice," "sauté," and "sweat" in the Glossary.

Ingredients

2 tablespoons olive oil
1/2 yellow onion, finely diced*
10 roasted Roma tomatoes, skinned and diced
1/2 teaspoon chopped* garlic
1/4 teaspoon curry powder
Granulated sugar
1 tablespoon sherry vinegar
Salt and pepper

CHIPOTLE SALSA

Makes 3-1/2 cups

For this simple salsa, grilling the tomatoes and onions is the way to achieve the right flavor. You can use more or less chile depending on your taste for spiciness. The salsa is a fine sidekick for Chilaquiles (recipe, p. 35) and tacos and a great topping for eggs and omelets, grilled meats, chicken, and a whole lot more.

What You Need

Grill   Food processor

How to Make

1. Grill* tomatoes, onions, and scallions.
2. Remove vegetables from the grill and cut into smaller pieces.
3. In the food processor, add chopped grilled vegetables, lime juice, cumin, cilantro, chiles, tomato juice, salt, and pepper. Blend until ingredients are well chopped and mixed.
4. Adjust for seasoning.

*See "chop" in the Glossary; for grilling, see Tips and Techniques.

Ingredients

10 Roma tomatoes, cut in half
1 small red onion, cut into slices
    1/3-inch thick
2 scallions, white and green
    parts, roughly chopped*
Juice of 3 limes
1/4 teaspoon ground cumin
1/2 cup chopped cilantro
2 small chipotle chiles
    (or more or less to taste)
1/2 cup tomato juice
Salt and pepper to taste

SALSA FRESCA

Makes 3 cups

This salsa adds a zingy freshness to many foods. Add more jalapeño if you want to make it spicier. The bright flavors may be tangy or mellow and sweet, depending on whether tomatoes are in season. The sweeter the tomato, the more rounded the salsa.

What You Need

Mixing bowl

How to Make

In the bowl, mix all ingredients well and let stand, covered, at room temperature for at least 1 hour. Refrigerate for longer storage.

*See "chop" and "dice" in the Glossary.

Ingredients

6 ripe tomatoes, diced* medium
1 small red onion, diced small
2 green onions, white and green parts, diced small
2 jalapeño chiles, seeded, ribs removed, and finely diced
1/2 cup chopped* cilantro
1/2 cup tomato juice
1/2 teaspoon ground cumin
2 tablespoons lemon juice
1 tablespoon salt

TOMATILLO SAUCE

Makes 2 cups

This refreshing salsa goes perfectly with Chilaquiles (recipe, p. 35), tacos, eggs and omelets, fish, chicken, and many other dishes. You could also pair it with hot tortilla chips for an appetizer or quick snack.

Tomatillos look like small green tomatoes with husks, but don't confuse them with green tomatoes. They're in the same family but are much tangier, tending toward sour.

What You Need

Standing blender

How to Make

1. In the blender, blend all ingredients until smooth. If necessary, blend in small batches.
2. Check for seasoning and serve right away, while the flavors are fresh and the sauce is a beautiful bright green.

*See "chop" and "smash" in the Glossary.

Ingredients

12 to 14 tomatillos, husked, washed, and cut in half
2 serrano chiles, chopped*
1/2 small yellow onion, chopped
2 garlic cloves, peeled and smashed*
1/2 cup chopped cilantro
1/4 cup water
Salt and pepper to taste

LEMON-BASIL AIOLI

Makes 1-1/4 cups

Aioli, the classic garlic mayonnaise, is a staple in Provence and is beloved by the French. I give it a bright twist here with fresh lemon and aromatic basil leaves. It's a perfect summer garnish.

What You Need

Food processor

How to Make

Put all ingredients into the food processor and purée well. If not using right away, transfer to a container with a tight-fitting lid and refrigerate. It will keep for up to 2 weeks.

Ingredients

1 cup mayonnaise
1 cup basil leaves, cleaned
3 tablespoons lemon juice
Salt and pepper to taste

TIPS AND TECHNIQUES

ARTICHOKES: Preparing artichokes can be time-consuming, but the process is easy and efficient once you've learned how to do it. Here are my methods for both baby and large artichokes.

Baby artichokes: When cleaning baby artichokes, cut about a quarter of the artichoke off the top (opposite the stem end) and then peel off the leaves until you reach the light yellow-green leaves near the center.

Trim the tough skin off the stem. Cut the artichoke in half, and if there are any reddish or pinkish leaves in the center, remove them. Place the cleaned artichoke hearts in a bowl with enough water to cover and the juice of 2 lemons.

At this point, you can make a delicious and simple dish with the raw artichokes by thinly shaving the artichokes and tossing them with shaved fennel, baby arugula, shaved Parmesan, olive oil, and lemon juice.

If you are going to cook the artichokes, braising is the best method; it helps them obtain maximum flavor. Steaming also works well. Here's how to braise baby artichokes.

What You Need

12-inch frying pan with lid

How to Make

1. Blot excess water off artichokes with a towel; they should be clean and dry.
2. Heat the skillet over medium-high heat and add oil. Add artichokes to the hot pan in a single layer. Let the artichokes get slightly browned, about 2 to 3 minutes, then add garlic, a pinch of chile flakes, and anchovies (if using) and stir.
3. Add wine and chicken stock. Cover and cook until the liquid is almost gone, about 15 minutes.
4. Add parsley, basil, a drop more of olive oil if needed, and the juice of 1 lemon. Salt and pepper to taste.

Large artichokes: The best way to cook these is by boiling or steaming. I like to flavor the water with bay leaves, olive oil, lots of salt, and lemons.

Cleaning large artichokes is basically about trimming. Cut a little bit off the stem and then slice off the top quarter of the artichoke. With kitchen shears, cut off the little thorn on each leaf. Be careful not to stick yourself — rubber

Ingredients

3 cups cleaned baby artichokes, halved
1/4 cup olive oil
1 tablespoon chopped garlic
Chile flakes
2 anchovy fillets, peeled and smashed (optional)
1 cup white wine (of a quality you'd like to drink)
1 cup Homemade Chicken Stock (recipe, p. 234) or water
3 tablespoons chopped parsley
2 tablespoons chopped fresh basil
Juice of 1 lemon
Salt and pepper

gloves may be helpful. Soak the cleaned, trimmed artichokes in a large container with water and lemon juice if you're not going to cook them right away

Fill a large pot halfway with water, flavor the water with 2 to 3 bay leaves, 1/4 cup olive oil, 2 tablespoons salt, and 2 lemons cut in half and then press in the artichokes stem side up. The artichokes should be completely submerged, so add more water if necessary. Lay wax paper over them and weigh them down with a heavy plate or a tight lid. Cook over medium heat for about 45 minutes or until fork-tender at the base. Remove from the pot and place on a sheet pan stem side up to let any excess water drain.

BLANCHING: This is a great way to partially cook foods that you plan to reheat later or use in salads. If done correctly, vegetables retain their vibrant color.

How to blanch: In a 4-quart saucepan, bring water to a boil over medium-high heat, making sure you have more water than vegetables. Salt very well, with up to a tablespoon or more of salt. This seems like a lot of salt, but it won't permeate the food; instead, it will help preserve the bright color of the vegetables. When the water is boiling rapidly, add the vegetables. You want to maintain a high heat in the water so the vegetables will cook fast and have no time to become limp.

Cooking time depends on what you are blanching. Obviously, carrots will take longer than asparagus. The trick for every vegetable is to cook it only to the point that it is barely getting soft — anywhere from 3 to 7 minutes. The moment the vegetables soften, remove them from the pot and immediately plunge them into an ice bath (a bowl or sink filled with water and ice cubes). This shocks the vegetables, helping them to cool rapidly as well as retain color.

CLARIFIED BUTTER: This is butter with the milk solids removed so that only the clear fat is left behind. The easiest way to make clarified butter is to slowly melt the butter over low heat. When it is completely melted and slightly foamy, remove from heat and let stand for 15 minutes. At this point, all the clear liquid should be at the bottom of the pan. Skim the top, removing any foam or solids that aren't clear oil; then carefully ladle out and reserve all the clear oil. Make sure not to stir up the liquid at the bottom, which you can discard after harvesting the clear liquid. Clarified butter keeps for up to 2 months in the refrigerator.

CLEANING MUSSELS AND CLAMS: Cleaning is necessary to eliminate sand and remove unwanted material, like the beards on the mussels. Wash the shellfish thoroughly and then soak in cold water, using about 2 tablespoons of salt and 2 tablespoons of cornmeal to 1/2 gallon of water. Let sit in the refrigerator for at least 2 to 3 hours; then rinse again and use.

CODDLING: This is the process of soft boiling eggs to lightly cook the yolks before using them in a dressing. Simply bring water to a simmer and add the whole eggs. Cook for about 4 minutes and then remove from the water. Crack open the shells and take out the yolk with a small spoon.

CUTTING ON THE BIAS: This means to cut vegetables at an angle. I believe this method is better than cutting straight up and down because longer, slender cuts help vegetables cook quicker and more evenly in a frying pan or wok. Bias cuts also make vegetables look great in salad, pastas, and other dishes

Lay the vegetable flat. Place your knife at a 30-degree angle and cut slender pieces about 2-1/2 to 3 inches in length. The more uniform the cuts, the better.

DEVEINING: Typically done with prawns or shrimp, this refers to the removal of the black digestive tract running down the middle of the prawn's back. Just make a light cut down the back of the prawn, and you will notice a black stringy thing. Remove it, discard, and then rinse the prawn well. Deveining prawns or shrimp is very important because prawns with their digestive tracts intact have an unappetizing appearance.

FLUFFING AN OMELET: Do this by pushing the cooked edges of the omelet toward the middle of the pan with a small rubber spatula and tilting the pan with a swirling, circular motion to move the raw egg to the edges of the pan.

FRESH WHIPPED CREAM: Using fresh whipped cream makes a world of difference to whatever you serve with it. With a whisk or a hand-held beater, whip 1 cup of heavy whipping cream — preferably not ultra-pasteurized — with 2 tablespoons of powdered sugar until the cream mounds into soft peaks. I don't make my whipped cream too sweet because I don't want it to be overpowering, but if you prefer sweeter cream, just add more powdered sugar. To get the fluffiest cream in the shortest amount of time, place the beaters and bowl in the freezer and take them out just before you're ready to whip the cream.

FRYING: This is the technique of cooking foods, with or without batter or coating, in hot oil. When done properly, it is one of the most delicious ways to prepare a wide range of foods. Here are some tips:

- A small electric deep-fryer with a basket is the easiest way to fry because it has a built-in thermometer that regulates the oil temperature.
- If you fry in a pot or a deep skillet, you'll need a cooking thermometer, and you'll have to control the temperature by adjusting the heat. Frying in a deep skillet has its advantages because you do not completely

submerge the food in oil, and by using the lid, you can steam and fry at the same time. This frying method works best with chicken and larger pieces of pork.

- When frying, always be sure your surroundings are safe. Keep an organized, uncluttered work station. Make sure there are no pots with water nearby, because when water hits hot oil, the oil splatters everywhere. Also, keep small children out of the kitchen.

- Many different oils yield excellent deep-fried foods. Peanut oil is the best flavorwise and doesn't burn very easily, but it can be expensive. California rice bran oil or grapeseed oil are also excellent; they're light and can handle very high temperatures. Vegetable oils, such as canola and corn, and hydrogenated fats such as Crisco work well, too, and are very affordable. Do not use heavy oils such as olive oil as they burn at a lower heat and will result in a very greasy final product.

GRILLING: This is a big topic that could use another book all its own, but here are some basic pointers:

- Always keep the grill at medium-high heat, about 350F to 375F. If it's too hot, it will burn everything; if it's too low, you will not achieve the slightly charred flavor that makes grilled foods so delicious.

- Know the hot spots on the grill as well as the places that aren't as hot. It's always good to get your initial grill marks by cooking over the hot spot; then, when you turn the food, rotate the pieces to a cooler part of the grill. This method is especially important when cooking big pieces of meat or bone-in chicken. When cooking chicken with the bone in, I move the pieces to the very edge of the grill so they won't get too dark.

- With a charcoal or mesquite grill, it's important to cover the food with the lid. This helps permeate the food with a smoky flavor and radiate heat evenly. Do not just cover the grill and leave it alone. Food on the grill must be checked and rotated constantly.

- Adjust the heat flow by opening or closing the vent on top of the lid. If you're using a gas grill, you can obtain a smokier flavor by putting dampened wood chips in a hot pan to one side of the grill and then covering the grill with the lid.

- Never put the final glaze or barbecue sauce on meat or chicken until it's just about done. This is the biggest mistake I see — people burning their food on the grill. Put the glaze or sauce on the food only at the end, so it becomes lightly caramelized from the heat.

- When grilling vegetables, the key is to make sure all the pieces are cut flat and large enough so they don't fall through the grill. For asparagus, lay them across the grate and roll them as they're cooking. Always use a brush to make sure vegetables are lightly but thoroughly coated with olive oil. Too much oil will make them taste like kerosene, but if you don't use enough, they won't cook evenly. Season the vegetables well while they're cooking so the seasoning penetrates the vegetables. Lay them out on a sheet pan when done. Do not stack them, or they will overcook.

POACHING: This is the technique of cooking foods in simmering water or broth. It produces lovely results with chicken, fish, and eggs and is a healthful technique because no oil or butter is used and any fat in the food melts away into the liquid.

Here are my poaching tips:

- When cooking chicken or fish, use a poaching liquid seasoned with herbs or vegetables. Chicken stock, wine, or clam juice dramatically increases flavor. Let the flavoring ingredients simmer in the broth for about 15 minutes before adding the chicken or fish.

- Always simmer the food rather than boiling it. Let it cook gently. Lift poached foods carefully with a slotted spoon and check for doneness. If the fish or chicken breast feels slightly firm, it should be done; this usually takes 10 to 12 minutes.

- When poaching eggs, bring water to a low simmer, add just a drop of white vinegar, crack the eggs into the liquid, and gently poach for 3 minutes. Remove with a slotted spoon.

- Fruit takes beautifully to poaching as well. Add 1 part granulated sugar to 4 parts water and flavor the water with anise, cinnamon, wine, or honey.

ROASTING GARLIC: This is one of the most useful accent foods and is so simple to make. Put 2 cups of peeled garlic cloves with the bottom stems cut off in a small ovenproof pan, such as cast iron or pottery, and pour in 1 cup of olive oil. On the stovetop, heat the pan over medium-low heat until the oil just starts to bubble; then place it in a 300F oven. Stir occasionally and let the garlic roast for about 20 minutes or until the cloves are golden brown and soft. Remove from the oven and let the cloves continue to steep in the oil until the oil is cool. Strain the oil and save for making salad dressing or dipping bread.

ROASTING PEPPERS: Roasting peppers, whether they're green, red, or yellow bell peppers or any variety of fresh chile, maximizes their flavors and makes it easier to remove the skin and seeds. You can do this either in a very hot oven or over a grill or gas burner. Here's how to do it:

- In the oven: Rub a very small amount of olive oil on the peppers. Place them in a roasting pan in a 500F oven until the peppers blister, about

15 minutes. Take them out and place them in a bowl, cover tightly with plastic wrap, and let sit for 1 hour. They will continue to steam, making the blistered skin easier to remove. Take off the plastic and let the peppers sit for 15 more minutes. At this point, they should be cool enough to peel. Do not run them under water because that will wash all the flavor away. Just rub away the skin with your thumb and then cut open and scrape out the seeds with a paring knife.

- On the grill: Lightly toss peppers with olive oil and char evenly on all sides for about 12 to 15 minutes. Place in a bowl and repeat steps above.

ROUX: To make a roux, cook flour with butter until it becomes soft and paste-like, of a consistency that would melt into your soup or sauce. A variation would be to cook the roux slowly, to brown and darken it. The darker it gets, the nuttier the final flavor will be. Roux is easy to burn, so it does take some practice to make the kind of dark roux that's the basis for New Orleans–style gumbo.

For a basic roux, melt 1/4 pound (1 stick) of butter in a 10-inch frying pan over low heat. With a wooden spoon, stir in 1 cup of flour, making sure to incorporate all the flour. Stir the mixture constantly until it forms a paste. Cook the paste for 2 more minutes. It should look golden, moist, and well blended.

SCORING: To score foods, run a knife across the surface to create a crisscross pattern. This is one way to help heat penetrate more quickly, which results in a crispier final product. Scoring typically is done to fish, duck breast, and pork with the skin on. Lightly run the blade of your knife at a slight angle in a crisscross pattern on the skin of the fish, duck, or pork, cutting only the skin, not the flesh. If you're scoring fish, make sure the scales have been removed.

TOASTING: Lightly toasting seeds or nuts brings the natural oils to the surface, resulting in maximum flavor. The simplest way is to lay the nuts or seeds in a single layer on a cookie sheet and bake at 350F until fragrant and lightly browned, about 10 minutes.

GLOSSARY

ACHIOTE: A paste made from achiote seeds used to flavor many Latin-inspired dishes. It adds a vibrant reddish orange color and tangy flavor and typically is used in marinades for fish, chicken, and pork. It can be purchased at any Mexican grocery store.

CARAMELIZE: The process of slow-cooking foods until the natural sugars are released and brown the surfaces. The word typically refers to onions. Perfect caramelized onions result from slow-cooking in unsalted butter over medium-low heat, stirring every few minutes until they turn a rich brown color and become very soft, about 15 to 20 minutes. This same method can be used with other vegetables and fruits, such as fennel bulbs or apples.

CHIFFONADE: To cut leafy herbs into very thin strips or ribbons. The finished product looks like a very fine julienne. This technique produces a beautiful garnish for your plates. For a chiffonade of basil, simply stack whole leaves tightly and run your knife across them, cutting the basil into strips the width of a string.

CHOLULA HOT SAUCE: I love to use this commercial hot sauce because of its sweet, tangy, and almost smoky flavor. The taste is wonderfully complex rather than fiery hot.

CHOP: This refers to several ways of cutting food. "Chop" means a simple uniform cut that is used with lettuce, vegetables like chard or other greens, and fruit. Simply run your knife across the vegetable or fruit in a uniform pattern. "Rough chop" means cutting into random chunks 1 to 2 inches in size. I use rough chopping for ingredients that will go into stocks, puréed soups, or sauces. Finely chopped ingredients are cut much smaller, about the size of confetti.

DEGLAZE: The technique of pouring wine, spirits, stock, or water into a pan in which food has been cooked. The liquid lifts up and incorporates the residue on the bottom of the pan, such as caramelized meat juices and bits of meat or skin. Deglazing makes your final product, such as a sauce, even more complex by using all the flavors that have become concentrated on the bottom of the pan.

DICE: This term appears in most recipes. For regular dice, food is cut into approximately 1/2-inch pieces; small dice means about 1/4-inch pieces; and fine dice is about half of that, almost as small as confetti. Whatever size you use, try to keep the pieces as uniform as possible. The more practice you have, the better and faster you will become at it.

DREDGE: To coat a piece of food very well with flour or seasoning so that it is completely covered.

GRANA PADANO: Similar to Parmesan, this one of my favorite cheeses. In flavor, it is sharp, nutty, and slightly salty, with a little sweetness at the end.

JULIENNE: The technique of cutting meat, chicken, or vegetables into very thin strips that are uniform in size. For vegetables, a French or Japanese mandoline works very well.

PAM COOKING SPRAY: A vegetable oil–based spray for coating pans, grills, and griddles so that food does not stick.

PARMESAN: A hard, sharp Italian cheese made from skim milk, it can be used alone for accenting dishes such as pasta and will add more flavor to any of your favorite recipes. The best Parmesans are marked Parmigiano-Reggiano and are imported from Italy.

REDUCE: To cook down the amount of liquid in a pan so that what's left is concentrated in flavor and texture. I typically reduce over medium-low heat so as not to burn the bottom of the pan. Depending on the recipe, you can reduce slightly or reduce all the way down until the liquid becomes a syrup.

RICOTTA SALATA: Dry, salted ricotta cheese that's semi-hard and has a sharp, tangy flavor. It grates beautifully and is used as a garnish for both hot dishes and salads.

SAMBAL: A spicy ground chile paste used to accent Asian or Southeast Asian–inspired dishes. I use it sparingly because too much can be overpowering. Sambal can be found in any Asian market.

SAUTÉ: To quick-cook foods over medium-high heat. Generally, you need a burner that puts out good heat and a long-handled skillet that's light enough to maneuver easily. Having a hot pan and working fast is the best way to sear and flavor your food. Deglazing the pan afterward with wine or whiskey brings the resulting sauce to a new level.

SIMMER: To cook gently over constant, low heat. The liquid will move or bubble quietly but should never reach what's called a "rolling boil," when the water boils rapidly and produces lots of big bubbles.

SMASH: To use the side of your knife to smash foods like garlic, anchovies, or capers into a paste. Just push down with the side of your knife and smear the food on the board, then chop it a little. Repeat this process until the food reaches a paste-like consistency.

SWEAT: The process of cooking raw vegetables just to the point that they become hot and their juices begin to emerge in the pan. Sweating onions means to cook them until they start to become translucent and soften.

THAI CURRY PASTE: Fresh bottled or packaged curry, moist and loaded with flavor and heat depending on the one you choose. Yellow Thai curry is the mildest, and red is the hottest. Even in small quantities, the complex flavors of Thai curry paste enhance many dishes. You can find Thai curry paste at any Asian market.

WHITE WINE WORCESTERSHIRE SAUCE: Lea & Perrins White Wine Worcestershire Sauce adds body and depth to chicken and fish, soups, and chowders. The white wine base is light enough that it doesn't overpower the natural flavors of the food. Original Worcestershire is great with any red meat.

INDEX

NOTES

NOTES

NOTES

NOTES

NOTES

NOTES

NOTES

NOTES